HOW TO BE OXBRIDGE

By the same author

Martin Allen Is Missing
Mad About the Boy

HOW TO BE
OXBRIDGE
⟦ *A Bluffer's Handbook* ⟧

Anton Gill

Illustrated by ffolkes

GRAFTON BOOKS

A Division of the Collins Publishing Group

LONDON GLASGOW
TORONTO SYDNEY AUCKLAND

To my parents,
neither of whom
went near Oxbridge

Grafton Books
A Division of the Collins Publishing Group
8 Grafton Street, London W1X 3LA

Published by Grafton Books 1985

British Library Cataloguing in Publication Data

Gill, Anton
How to be Oxbridge: a bluffer's handbook
1. University of Oxford – Anecdotes, facetiae,
satire, etc. 2. University of Cambridge –
Anecdotes, facetiae, satire, etc. 3. Oxford
(Oxfordshire) – Social life and customs –
Anecdotes, facetiae, satire, etc. 4. Cambridge
(Cambridgeshire) – Social life and customs –
Anecdotes, facetiae, satire, etc.
I. Title
378.425′74′0207   LF522

ISBN 0–246–12432–6

Set by Fakenham Photosetting Limited
Fakenham, Norfolk
Printed in Great Britain
at the University Press, Cambridge

Contents

Preface

IT IS EASY to establish Oxbrites. They *know* they are good, so that even if their careers in the World Outside fail abysmally, they carry with them none of the anxious desire to please that infects ordinary mortals. This self-confidence (and do not be deceived; it is there even in the most neurotic and insecure Oxbrite who has stood the course) is reflected in their manner, their mode of speech (less an accent than a way of using language), their interests and even their neuroses, and it sets them apart. This set of values is not easily acquired: nearly every Oxbrite has to adopt the so-called Oxbridge 'mask' during term time when he is 'up', and some never ever manage to do without it again. The 'mask' is essentially a front, a persona which you project to give the impression that you are more fully in control of the situation than in fact you are. In the end, most Oxbrites find that pretence and reality fuse, and they can discard the mask for good – at least in their conscious minds.

The 'mask' breeds a good deal of pseudery among Oxbrites when they are 'up'; for example, one Cambridge Oxbrite used to impress his friends by always being able to identify any record that happened to be playing in their rooms as he walked in. He was finally rumbled when someone left a record sleeve ostentatiously out that was *not* related to the music playing. The worst example of intellectual pseudery in reminiscence which the author has been able to isolate occurs in Leonard Woolf's autobiography, *Sowing*: 'late at night in the May [*sic*] term, I like to remember, Lytton, Saxon, Thoby Stephen,

Clive Bell, and I would sometimes walk through the Cloisters of Nevile's Court in Trinity and looking through the bars at the end on to the willows and water of the Backs, ghostly in the moonlight, listen to the soaring song of innumerable nightingales. And sometimes as we walked back through the majestic Cloisters we chanted poetry. More often than not it would be Swinburne.'

The 'mask' also breeds the phenomenon of 'secret work'. As work is now *in*, this curiosity is only of historical (pre-1975) interest. Its objective was to show that you could sail through exams without effort. Some really could – 'A.A.' was a brilliant Oxbrite who read Medicine and Philosophy simultaneously, and got Firsts in both. He spent the night before his finals began at a ball in London; 'A.A.' was so exceptional, though, that he once read *and digested* three Thomas Mann novels in one night. Those who could not perform these feats but wished to appear to, resorted to 'secret work' – something to be done in the dead hours of the Oxbridge day, 2 a.m.–12 noon. However carefully work was performed in this manner, suspicion was quickly aroused:

'What were you doing yesterday morning at 10 a.m.?'

'Um – having a cocktail with Melanie, and "Lockjaw" Harrison.'

'Are you sure? I thought I saw you going into the UL.' ... and so on.

A good rule of thumb by which to recognize Oxbrites concerns garrulity and indecision. Nearly all Oxbrites talk too much (a habit which has perhaps become a tradition, deriving from when examinations were conducted orally in the form of Disputations – books and writing materials in those days being expensive and scarce), and they also avoid where possible talking to the point. Perhaps as a result of this, Oxbrites are not often 'doers'. A true Oxbrite is unlikely to have the *nous* to set up, or make a go of, his own business; indeed, he would consider such enterprise vulgar. He will, however, make a very good 'lieutenant', or 'right-hand man' in a business, where the absolute initiative does not lie with him.[1] The natural habit of Oxbrites (non-scientists) is to let their punt drift down the river of life, occasionally and idly dipping their hands into the water – though this is less true of the younger (under 35) Oxbrites today, as liberalism and competition force those who are 'up' to become less like undergraduates and more like common students.

Most Oxbrites enjoy irony, and take especial delight in using it on people who don't understand. Be warned.

In these days of greater democracy, at least on a cosmetic level, Oxbridge is a changing institution. When this book is published, all but one of the previously male Oxbridge colleges will have become co-residential, only the women's colleges (and not all of *them*) holding on to the fine old tradition of one college, one sex. Fewer and fewer Sebastian Flyte lookalikes are to be seen swanning round the quads of Hertford, and even the brief Brideshead wave that swept over Oxford in 1981–2 in the wake of the tv-series-based-on-the-novel has crashed onto the shore of memory – for that tv series is now a whole generation away in Oxbridge terms.

There is less and less an Oxbridge type who is moulded before he arrives. This means that men, and public school men in particular, no longer have the upper hand. Such people, used to the rigours of boarding school, found nothing to jib at in freezing rooms, appalling food and mediaeval plumbing. Today's generation of Oxbrites, especially the women undergraduates, are making more demands. One of the results of this is that loos are being repaired, and new ones are even being built. Cafeterias haven't *replaced* Hall, but they sit cheek-by-jowl with the

---

[1] This premise cannot be applied so easily to female Oxbrites, who tend to be more aggressively ambitious than their male counterparts, having had to fight harder, earlier, for what they've got.

older form of feeding, and where the stuff on the table is not up to scratch, Hall comes off worse. Even the ghastliness of beans on toast in your rooms does not beat the ghastliness of a grey and watery stew, served on oak in a dim room twice the size of the average village church, and usually twice as cold.

To return to the Flyte-type. He may be fading, but the manner and custom which bred him are not. Even in a modern college like Churchill you will find him perversely entrenched, despite all the efforts of the liberal-Marxist dons. This manner and this custom must be learnt, if you are to pass yourself off as, and thus into the circles of, Oxbrites. They are subtle things, but they so influence undergraduates that, be their former background Scottish estate or Birmingham slum, at the end of their three to four years at Oxbridge they will bear a certain stamp.[1] This book gives its diligent readers all the information they will need to know in order to pass themselves off as Oxbridge, and thus to enjoy all the privileges and favours life confers on those who really are.[2] Readers are, however, very strongly advised to familiarize themselves with the Glossary before plunging in, as the use of obscure and arcane words from the word 'go'[3] is quite inevitable. Would-be Oxford Oxbrites should further note the habit there of abbreviating certain street-names: High Street becomes 'the High'; Broad Street, 'the Broad'; Cornmarket, 'the Corn', and so on. *But* note that not *all* streets are subject to this. Never refer to St Aldate's, for example, as 'the Ald'; and it is archaic to refer to St Giles' as 'Giler' nowadays.

---

[1] Unless of course they read one of the more monstrously dull sciences – for more on this, see Subjects: In & Out, pp. 51–2.

[2] If any – but that's another story.

[3] Not to mention 'Little Go'.

Acknowledgements

MANY PEOPLE HELPED with this book, offering anecdotes and reminiscences, and delving into what were often excruciatingly painful memories. There is no room to name them all here, and *one* actively and urgently requested anonymity.

Here are some of those who did not, and to whom I owe a special debt of gratitude: Lindsay Anderson; Jay Andrews; Sally Angel; Anne Charvet; John Collett; Cathy Collis; Arthur Crisp; Alan Dingle; Alan Frank; Paul Gambaccini; Nicola Gill; Bevis Hillier; Jennie James; Terry James; Richard Johnson; Leslie Kingsland; Anne de Lara; Jeremy Leighton; Sue Leighton; Miranda Long; Harry Loshak; George Lucas; Gerald McAuliffe; the late Anthony Masters; Revd Richard Minter; Clive Newton; Elaine Paintin; Reuben Peck; H. C. Porter; Kathy Rowan; Jonathan Sage; John Scotney; Patrick Scott; Kevin Sim; Victor Smart; Revd Paul Smythe; Joe Steeples; J. V. Stevenson; Anthony Vivis; Michael Walsh; Stephen Warren; Stephen White; Peter Windows and Polly Woodman. Belated thanks to Roger Croucher and Barry de Lara; and to Sam and Peaches, who kept me company.

Extra special thanks are due to E. L. Gill, for additional academic and historical research; and to Mark Lucas, without whom . . .

I would also like to thank the staff of the University Library, Cambridge; the British Library, London; the Bodleian Library, Oxford; and the College of Arms.

[1]

The Background

NO MATTER HOW you look at it, having been to Oxford or Cambridge confers advantages on those fortunate enough to have done so which other universities simply cannot match. Even being a self-made man, or a rough, industrial northerner, is as nothing compared with the comfortable permanence of those confident words, 'when I was up at Oxford' (or, of course, Cambridge). No other university in the world, not Harvard, not London, not Paris, carries such clout, or confers membership of a more exclusive club. There is, of course, no reason at all why just a few people alone should enjoy this privilege. You can put anything you like on your curriculum vitae, secure in the knowledge that nobody will ever check the facts there. However, what you must be able to do is back up what you've written down with expert bluff – like the double agent who has to learn a new identity. If you've pretended to have been to Oxbridge, it is crucial that you know the associated folklore, or you will be found out when you are confronted by people who really went there. The task is further complicated by the fact that all Oxbrites are expert bluffers themselves, running a lot of their lives on the premise, 'if you don't know it, busk it'. A famous Oxbridge anecdote concerns two Oxbrites earnestly discussing the most recent Bergman film about which controversy raged at the time. They argued about it fiercely and in detail for a whole evening, and it was only some time later that *each* discovered that the other had not actually *seen* it. Busking on this level, of course, cannot be taught: it can only come with experience; but you can find one or two simple ploys designed to be adapted to most circumstances in Chapter 4: Arrival.

Two choices immediately face you: which university, and what college.

Subject used to have a lot to do with which university you chose. It was Oxford for Humanities, Cambridge for Sciences. True, Oxford was a bit old-fashioned, but it had élan, albeit a rather vulgar élan. It had given its name not only to a city and a university, but also to 21 United States towns, a Morris car, bags, marmalade, grey, toecaps, a Group, a Movement and an accent, as well as a dictionary and several Books of . . . On the other hand, you had to pass an exam in at least one classical language to get *into* a Humanities school. Sciences were big in the late fifties and early sixties, thanks largely to the efforts of such pro-nuclear Oxbrites as C. P. Snow, but it wasn't long before people realized that they were rather a bore after all – you had to go to lectures, and you spent the *other* half of your time in the labs, so there wasn't any time left to do any of the important things that Oxbrites like doing – e.g. putting an Austin car on the roof of the Senate House, or filling yourself with champagne and roaring up and down the High in great mobs, with the Oxford Constabulary in hot pursuit. Also, it was relatively easy to get a place to read for a science degree, and therefore not at all dashing. The most popular faculty at Oxbridge in the mid to late sixties was the English faculty at Cambridge, which was the hardest of any to get into, and also boasted the highest suicide rate. Truly a challenge. The death-blow to Sciences was dealt when it was discovered that Margaret Thatcher had read Chemistry at Somerville (Oxon.). The author cannot imagine why. Nowadays, with a few exceptions, the ranks of scientific Oxbrites are made up of gnomes (Oxon.), or grey men (Cantab.): they are too busy working to be amongst those who Make Things Happen.

Today, Oxford has blown some of its cobwebs off, and

on the roof

Cambridge has ceased to be quite as aggressively high-tech as it once was, when Crick found out about the Double Helix, and quit his fellowship of Churchill when the college was given £30,000 to build a chapel, which he thought was an 'expensive anachronism'. So, choose according to your taste: your choice of college will probably be more important anyway, though you must never forget that although it is pooh-poohed a good deal these days, the old Oxford and Cambridge rivalry still exists, and Oxbrites (Oxon.)[1] will feel vaguely offended if they are taken for Oxbrites (Cantab.), and vice versa. It is a rivalry of equals, however, since Oxbridge looks down on everywhere else; but when you join the Oxbridge mafia in the World Outside, beware: you will find that one or other university more or less dominates different professions, or sections of professions. More on this in Chapter 16: Life After Oxbridge.

Oxbrites call themselves different names. Oxford people like to call themselves *Oxonians*. Before the advent of women, which has led of course to a lot of confusion, they called themselves Oxford *men*, or more particularly Wadham men, or Lincoln men or whatever. Cambridge people may call themselves *Cantabrians*, or, if they want to be picky and mediaeval, *Cantabrigians*, but they generally stick to Cambridge men (or, now, women, though that never sounds quite right): see more below. As nearly all the colleges now take both men and women the situation is complicated these days, and it is still, after twelve years or so of co-residence, pretty non-U to have been at an erstwhile women's college if you are a man, and vice versa. The most important thing, in life after Oxbridge, is *never to volunteer the information that you were at Oxbridge* (except on cvs): such vulgarity belongs to the type of person who boasts about his red Maserati to a girl, or who has a

[1] The noun 'Oxbrite' used in this book is unisex; where necessary it is qualified with an adjective of gender.

cocktail bar in his drawing room or a 'personalized' number plate on his car. Be modest. Understate. Let the information slip unintentionally, and then blush furiously. Or just let it be drawn out of you reluctantly. The greater your ability to understate, the greater your chances are of impressing, always provided that you *do* get the information across. And remember, don't begin by saying 'I was at Oxbridge', but 'I was at Trinity/John's/ Pembroke ...'; the name of the college and the assumed knowledge of where it is are more important than mentioning the university itself. Indeed, people who go on about how they were at Oxbridge, especially celebrities, often lay themselves open to the suspicion that they in fact *weren't*. Genuine Oxbrites more often than not deprecate the time they were up, 'Considering how privileged we were meant to have been, and what a good time we were all meant to be having, it's surprising how wretched we felt for most of the time.' And this, of course, is a lot closer to the truth.

Oxford is more boastful and more open than Cambridge. You could say that Cambridge is to Oxford as Paris is to New York. This is partly owing to the fact that Oxford is a little older and has more vulgar cachet, but also to the fact that Oxford is on a well-trodden tourist route, and that the Town is just as important as the Gown, thanks to Lord Nuffield in recent years. The university has been called the Latin Quarter of Oxford. In Cambridge the university has no such identity crisis; it dominates easily. Oxford colleges huddle, and turn their backs to the busy main streets. Cambridge colleges are open, airy and confident. At Cambridge, only one college charges admission to tourists. At Oxford, three do. Part of Oxford's ancient insecurity is borne out by the University Arms, which feature an open book on which its well-known motto is inscribed: DOMINUS ILLUMINATIO MEA. The Cambridge Arms also have a book in the middle of the shield. It is closed, and whereas everybody knows Oxford's motto, even Cambridge undergraduates don't know theirs (it's HINC LUCEM ET POCULA SACRA). Cambridge refers to 'the book which is always open at the same page'; Oxford refers to 'the book which is never opened at all'.

Sparing you for a moment the hideous pitfalls that the names of Heads of Houses can present (at Cambridge they're nearly all Masters, but at Oxford there's a confusing plethora of Provosts, Rectors, Wardens and Deans as well) the first basic difference to be learnt is the names of the terms in the academic year. Most sensible institutions go for Autumn, Easter (or Spring) and Summer. You'll be familiar with them if you went to an ordinary school. This is not the case at Oxbridge. At Oxford, you'll have to cope with Michaelmas, Hilary and Trinity. Michaelmas is OK, public schools use that, but be on your guard when faced with 'Didn't I last see you in Hilary?', because it doesn't mean what it seems to (although of course it might do); and 'the Ball will be held in Trinity' may mean the term rather than the college (of the same name, and there's one at Cambridge, too). At Cambridge you'll be confronted with Michaelmas and Lent (also used by some public schools), but the Summer term is called *Easter*. Term lasts ten weeks or so; but within it is *Full* Term, when people get down to the real nitty gritty. Full Term lasts eight weeks.

The next thing to deal with is Antiquity. Both universities are old, but both have claimed to be considerably older than they are. Oxford kicks off with a claim to have been founded by the mythical King Memphric in 1000 BC; Cambridge had a stab at foundation by a Prince Cantaber, a Spaniard living at Athens, in the 'year of the world' 4321, and the Suffolk poet John Lydgate says that Julius Caesar took some Cambridge people back to Rome with him after he'd

6

'Didn't I last see you in Hilary?'

conquered Britain. Much later, and in order to win a lawsuit, the dons of University College, Oxford, forged some deeds (in 1381) to prove the college's foundation by Alfred the Great. This is now politely known as the Aluredian Legend, and is equally spurious.

In fact, no one founded either place. Both began with groups of students gathering around teachers in the twelfth century. They began because a number of English students were kicked out of the University of Paris in 1167 (Henry II stirring things, no doubt). These students were settled in Oxford by 1200, and in 1209 some of them fled to Cambridge after fighting with the townspeople (a tradition nobly preserved, and continuing today). They chose Cambridge because the place was already a centre of learning, based around Ely Cathedral, Barnwell Priory and the convent of St Radegund.

There were for some time no colleges at all at either university. The students lived in lodgings, or lived rough in shanty towns. They created lots of friction with the townspeople, and things went from bad to worse until finally someone called William of Durham stumped up 310 marks to establish four scholars at University College, Oxford, in 1249. Cambridge had been licked into shape in 1231 by a rather querulous Henry III in response to reports of 'troublesome and rebellious clerks' from the Chancellor and Masters to the Bishop of Ely. Henry had had trouble with the prostitutes and the French students at Oxford at about the same time. He said that all clerks (students) *must* be under the tuition of a Master, and that rents must be assessed by two Masters and two townsmen, called 'taxors'. That office only lapsed in 1856. The Bishop of Ely, Hugh de Balsham, founded the first Cambridge college, Peterhouse, in 1284. The rest is history.

Women, of course, didn't come until much later, at least in any academic sense. Brothels were controlled by the Oxbridge authorities from the Middle Ages to the nineteenth century, when the responsibility came to be thought unseemly. Women undergraduates arrived in Cambridge first, when Emily Davies opened a college for women in 1869. It moved to Girton (a decorous two miles out of town) in 1873. Newnham, the second women's college, opened in 1878.

From 1881 onwards at Cambridge, women were actually allowed to sit the Tripos examination, but of course they couldn't take *degrees*. They weren't allowed to do *that* until 1923, and even then they were only granted titular degrees. The first fully-fledged woman graduate was the Queen Mother, who was granted an honorary degree in 1947. From 1948 the rest of the monstrous regiment was fully admitted, and in 1952 the final bastion crumbled, and women's colleges achieved equal status with men's. At Oxford the situation was similar. Degrees for women were first granted in 1920, when they also became full members of the university; but it wasn't until 1959 that their colleges were granted the same status as men's. Once in, they made up for lost time. Cambridge had its first woman Vice-Chancellor (or boss) in 1975; the first lady proctor arrived on the scene in Oxford in 1979. Headgear then became a problem, since the soft black cap worn by women cannot be raised in ceremonial greetings. Thus it was that women took to wearing the hard 'mortar board' (actually called a 'cap', but called a 'square' at Cambridge) which hitherto had adorned male heads only. Nowadays you don't see them at all much, except on ceremonial occasions, but Oxford undergraduates have to have them *with* them when they matriculate, and when they sit exams. Only they don't have to *wear* them. More on this vexed question appears later, in Chapter 5: Vita Academica and Chapter 10: Dress Sense. Women have had a raw deal at Oxbridge, especially as a good number of colleges, right back to 1326, were founded by them.

Their revenge is that they have become the lifelong obsession of all Oxbridge men, deprived of them for three years in their early twenties.

So: choose your university with care, and according to your taste. Oxford is townier and busier; Cambridge is much prettier (despite recent attempts by Town and Gown to turn the city centre into a glass-and-concrete nightmare), off the beaten track, and doesn't quite match up to Oxford's heavyweight (but unreliable) literary and political heritage. In after-life, Cambridge people can don suits and become Keen. Oxford people tend to stay in pullovers and cords, wear bow-ties, and look down on life in general.

[2]

The Colleges – a brief introduction

THE NEXT THING to tackle is the colleges you've chosen.
Although most are co-residential now, play it safe if you
are a man and only claim a college that was originally for
men only. Women needn't be so cautious, but take care:
Clare or King's or any other trendy college is smarter to
claim than St Catharine's or Selwyn, or even Christ
Church. Beware of saying that you were at Queens'
(Cantab.) when you mean The Queen's (Oxon.); don't
confuse Magdalene with Magdalen, and know how to
pronounce it. *Never* refer to New College simply as 'New',
and remember that St Edmund Hall isn't the same as St
Edmund's House. Lady Margaret Hall is an Oxford
college, once only for women and now co-residential. It's
commonly called LMH; but Lady Margaret Boat Club
(LMBC) is the boat club of St John's College, Cambridge.
Mercifully, a lot of the colleges in both universities have
the same name, but study the list which follows. Aids to
pronunciation and usage have been given to help you. Pay
strict attention to the titles of Heads of Houses, especially
at Oxford – it's no use referring to 'the Master of
Magdalen' (though of course it's quite correct to speak of
'the Master of Magdalene') – you'd be sunk before you
start. And don't claim, as one well-known Irish broad-
caster did recently, to have been offered a place as an
undergraduate at All Souls. The college doesn't take them.

Here is a list of the most important[1] Oxford and

---

[1] There are others; ignore them. You might as well have been to an
ordinary university. NB Lucy Cavendish, Cambridge, is *not* to be
confused with Lucy Clayton.

Cambridge colleges which *do* take undergraduates together with the essential facts you should know about them. Although a graduate college, All Souls is included in the list because it is famous, and because of the oddness of its inmates and its customs.[1] Colleges are mixed unless otherwise stated. For convenience, a grading system has been used:

$$✓✓ = \text{go}$$
$$✓ = \text{second choice}$$
$$✗ = \text{go if you have to}$$
$$✗✗ = \text{avoid.}$$

Ungraded colleges are *grey*. Any gastronomic comments are based on an averaged assessment of the various buffets, cafeterias, Halls, Formal Halls and Super Halls available. Formal Hall is better than Hall, and Super Hall is, well, super. Usually.

Oxford Colleges in Order of Foundation

✓✓ **University College.** Called 'Univ' or 'Univ, O' (by Rhodes scholars who need to establish their sense of place). Founded in 1279 (formally) by William of Durham, who had endowed it 30 years earlier. It is academically hot, most of its students get good rooms, and it has a good bar – though not cheap. Food is good, but the laundry is poor. The poet Shelley was here (he was sent down for atheism), and more recent alumni whose names are worth dropping are Richard Ingrams and Paul Gambaccini. *Once a grey college, now an in college, on account of its brightness.* Head of House (HoH): MASTER. Colours: navy and gold.

✓ **Balliol** was endowed between 1263–8 by John de

[1] More on All Souls in Chapter 8: Customs.

Balliol. Since the time of its most famous Master, Benjamin Jowett (1870–93), it has held a reputation for being academically very hot, but its list of famous alumni goes back further than Jowett, and includes John Evelyn, Adam Smith, Matthew Arnold and Hilaire Belloc, along with a good clutch of bishops and politicians. In the eighteenth century Lady Elizabeth Perriam donated 24 WCs to the place, 'to be not less than one hundred yards from the rooms'. It has no gate hours, but despite this and its late-night snack bar, its reputation as an *in* college is slipping. Name-droppable alumni include Harold Macmillan, Edward Heath and Roy Jenkins. Balliol entertains a traditional rivalry with Trinity, next door. Once, Trinity men blocked Balliol men into their own library with a giant snowball. In revenge, Balliol turfed Trinity's JCR. *Still good for clerical and political careers*. HoH: MASTER. Colours: navy, white and magenta.

✓**Merton** got going in Surrey in 1264 and moved to Oxford ten years later. It was founded by Walter de Merton, who also bought land at Cambridge since at first he couldn't make up his mind where to plant his college. It's academically warm, and its Hall serves (currently) the best food in the university, thanks to a generous endowment which pays the wages of a master chef – he gets more than the average don. Sheridan Morley, P. J. Kavanagh and Kris Kristofferson were here, and before them T. S. Eliot and Max Beerbohm. HoH: WARDEN. Colours: mauve and white. Scholars at Merton are called 'postmasters' by the way. *An* in *college.*

Exeter. Founded in 1314 by Walter de Stapledon. This one is on Turl Street, as are Lincoln and Jesus, and older alumni will be able to reminisce about terrific riots and battles between the colleges on the street. Exeter's traditional rivalry is with Jesus. Exeter men once caught some pigeons, fed them on Ex-Lax, and released them in Jesus during Hall. Alumni include J. R. R. Tolkien, and the actor Richard Burton. Exeter's Sweaty Discos are famous, and it runs a good Mini-Ball in Hilary during the Torpids (boat races); but despite everything, it's an *out* college, and anyway, if you say you were 'at Exeter', people will think you mean Exeter *University*, of which the less said the better. Even so, Exeter College specializes in West Country undergraduates. HoH: RECTOR. Colours: magenta and black.

✓ **Oriel.** Founded in 1326 by Adam de Brome, it is chiefly famous for rowing and for Cecil Rhodes, an alumnus who gave vast sums to his old college. One of the things he endowed was food, which is why it's better here than at most other places. The nutrition available at Oriel's table may also partly account for the college's astonishing success in rowing. It's heavy on sport and still has a high public school intake. It's an *in* college, all right, though rather a specialized one. Oriel was the last Oxford men's college to go co-residential, which it did at the beginning of the 1985 academic year. A mixed bag of alumni include Sir Walter Raleigh and A. J. P. Taylor. HoH: PROVOST. Colours: navy and white.

Queen's (or more properly, **The Queen's**) **College.** *Note where the apostrophe is!* Usually just called Queen's. The Queen in question was Philippa of Hainault, whose Cumbrian former chaplain, Robert de Eglesfield, founded this one in 1341. His drinking cup – an auroch's horn mounted on eagles' feet – is still used as a loving-cup on festive occasions, such as the ceremony of the Needle and Thread. They announce Hall here by blowing a trumpet, but the food hardly merits it. It's an easygoing college with special links with the North of England, whence a number of its undergraduates still come. Very pretty architecture (Wren and Hawksmoor), but by and large a *grey* college, redeemed by a chef reputedly paid *twice* what the average fellow gets. Alumni: Leopold Stokowski, Brian Walden, Rowan Atkinson. HoH: Provost. Colours: navy and white.

✓ **New College** was founded by Bishop William of Wykeham, who also founded Winchester School, in 1379, and not surprisingly it's full of Wykehamists. The good bishop got the site cheap, because it had been an ancient plague pit. Founder's kin can get special deals on entry, though it's hard to claim direct descent from a pre-Reformation bishop! If your name is Twistleton-Wykeham-Fiennes, though, and you know how to pronounce 'Fiennes', you may be in with a chance. The place has a good wine cellar, and the bar is rather romantically in the fourteenth-century vaults. Alumni include Maurice Bowra, Tony Benn, Lord Longford and John Fowles. A *problem* college, but not bad to have been to, especially if you were also at Winchester, and are aiming at the City (cf. Eton and King's). The college name is *never* shortened to just 'New', and it is the only college that *demands*, rather than supplicates, degrees from the university. HoH: Warden. Colours: brown and white.

Lincoln is small and tends to be sporty. It scores high on entertaining, and usually runs to an annual Ball. Within living memory it had the engaging habit of selling the wine it had laid down to its inmates at the price it was bought in for. But the obscurity of its name precludes it from being an *in* college. Good alumni include Sir Osbert Lancaster and John le Carré. HoH: Rector. Colours: navy and light blue.

All Souls. The College of All Souls of the Faithful Departed was run up by Henry Chichele, Archbishop of

Canterbury, in 1438, to commemorate those English who died during the Hundred Years War. It has no undergraduates, and the only duty required of the 50 fellows is to pray for the souls of the English dead of the Hundred Years War. They still do this from time to time. More on this remarkable institution, and what they get up to, later, Chapter 8: Customs. HoH: WARDEN.[1]

✓✓**Magdalen.** *Note the absence of an 'e' on the end.* Pronounced 'maudlin'. Founded by William of Waynflete in 1458. It is a rich and famous college, and undoubtedly *in*, though the five-hundred-year-old 'May Morning' tradition, at which at 6 a.m. on 1st May the choristers of Magdalen Choir School sing 'Te Deum Patrem Colimus' from the top of the Magdalen bell tower (followed by Morris dancing and heavy drinking), seems to be less enthusiastically followed these days. After all, it does mean either staying up all night, or getting up horribly early. Magdalen scholars are called 'demies' *not* because they only drink halves but because their allowance used to be half that of a fellow. Its food is average, and its public school intake is still relatively high. Alumni: Sir John Betjeman (sent down for failing his obligatory Divinity paper), Dudley Moore, Lord Denning, Oscar Wilde, C. S. Lewis, Sir Thomas Bodley and a host of others. Magdalen has had, astonishingly, only a dozen or so Presidents since its Foundation. The most famous must be Martin Routh, who died in 1854 at the age of 100, having been President for 63 years. HoH: PRESIDENT. Colours: black and white.

✓**Brasenose.** This one is often just called 'BNC'. It takes its name from a grotesque early mediaeval doorknocker, and was founded in 1509. In the late nineteenth century,

[1] The other graduate college worth mentioning here is Nuffield, simply because after Lord Nuffield had endowed it he used to refer to it as 'that bloody Kremlin where left-wingers study at my expense'.

the college was so heavily addicted to sport that 'no aesthete was safe' in it. One such who had to go there on a visit walked with two sticks, relying on the under-graduates' spirit of sportsmanship preventing them from attacking a 'lame' man. Now that the college is mixed, with a pretty equal male/female ratio, those sterling times have gone. Beer is good here, and living is cheap. Recommended, but not quite *in*. Alumni: William Golding, Robert Runcie, Michael Palin, Earl Haig, John Buchan, Walter Pater. HoH: PRINCIPAL. Colours: yellow and black.

Corpus Christi. There's one at Cambridge too. This one is smaller and younger, and tends to be academically hot, especially in Literae Humaniores. 'Corpus' hosts the annual inter-college tortoise races, and they actually are the high point of the inmates' year. Alumni: John Keble, William Waldegrave. HoH: PRESIDENT. Colours: navy and red (rather attractive). 'Corpus' was also the only Oxford college to give *none* of its plate to Charles I to help him fight Cromwell.

✓**Christ Church.** Known as Ch. Ch., or even Cha Cha, CCC, or, most usually, The House, but never openly called Christ Church *College*, it was first founded as Cardinal College by Wolsey in 1525. After his fall, Henry VIII refounded it with becoming modesty as Henry VIII College. When it got too ecclesiastical for his liking, he suppressed it again, only to refound it in 1546 (in a brilliant PR double-bill: he set up Trinity, Cambridge in the same year). It is one of the biggest and the second richest. It contains a cathedral. It used to be *in*, but recently its upper-crust heartiness and young fogey tendencies have become too much to bear, and now it is *out*. Women are allowed in these days, but a recent graffito declared 'A Woman's Place Is Not In The House', so the situation is uneasy. Claim it as your own if you are over 35, and if you move in legal or financial circles, but be careful: its graduates are beady. Fellows of this one are confusingly called Students. It has links with Westminster School, so if you can pull it off, tie yourself up with a 'Westminster and The House' background, and you should sail through. Some people from ordinary schools are now being allowed in. Christ Church is famous for 'Mercury' – a pool in the centre of Tom Quad decorated with a metal statue of the god, in which undesirables were until recently ducked by hearties – 'We put him in Mercury'. Tom Quad also boasts Tom Tower, which houses several bells (Dounce, Clement, Austin, Hautclere, Gabriel and John) of which the chief, Tom, is rung 101 times every evening at 9.05 p.m. – once for every member of the original foundation, and at 9.05 because Oxford is 1°15′ west of Greenwich, and therefore strictly speaking it is actually 9.00 p.m. at Oxford. Alumni include nearly every Prime Minister who ever lived, together with Auberon Waugh, Anthony Howard and Peter Jay, not to mention John Ruskin, 'Lewis Carroll' and W. H. Auden. HoH: DEAN. Colours: navy, scarlet, brown and white.

Trinity is a little younger and not nearly as famous as the Cambridge college of the same name. Its undergraduates are not best known for their intellect, but seem amiable enough in other ways. Jeremy Thorpe and Sir Kenneth Clark were here, as was Sir Richard Burton, the explorer and pornographer. He was sent down for duelling. HoH: PRESIDENT. Colours: navy and white.

✓**St John's** is the richest college, but that doesn't necessarily make it *in*. Good for drama, the St John's Mummers have plenty of money to shower on nascent theatrical talent. However, Cambridge is still the place to go if you want to Make It In The Theatre. It maintains links with Merchant Taylors' School, because its founder was a member of the Merchant Taylors' Company. The fellows are canny: Charles II once asked them for a wooden painting of his parents, which they reluctantly gave him; but when he airily said that in return they could have anything that it was within his power to give them, they asked for it back again. There's also a story that you can walk from John's Oxford to John's Cambridge without stepping off either's land (but cf. John's Cambridge). Academically the place is red hot, maintaining a strong lead in the annual Norrington Table (a kind of points sheet for measuring academic achievement in degree passes between the colleges). Alumni include Kingsley Amis and Philip Larkin. HoH: PRESIDENT. Colours: black, scarlet and yellow.

Jesus. There's another one of these at Cambridge, too. The place has always had strong links with Wales, which will of course automatically put it on a lot of people's *out* list – after all, no one wants to get crammed in with a bunch of leek-eaters. But with the Welsh Development Board merrily flogging the land of sheep and water for all it is worth at the moment you could do worse in an expanding provincial business than to claim membership of this college. Inconsistently its most famous alumni are Sir Harold Wilson and Beau Nash. HoH: PRINCIPAL. Colours: green and white.

✓**Wadham.** Still governed by the statutes of its foundation in 1612, this solid little college has an impressive list of alumni: Alan Coren, Michael Foot, Melvyn Bragg, Lindsay Anderson, Tony Richardson and George Devine – the last three ran the Royal Court Theatre in London for some time, though the Wadham connection was purely coincidental. HoH: WARDEN. Colours: black, gold and light blue.

✓✓ **Pembroke.** An *in* college by virtue of shooting up the Norrington Table from second-to-last in 1983 to second-from-top in 1984. It is a younger foundation than its Cambridge counterpart, and tends to live under the shadow of Christ Church across the road. Samuel Johnson was here for four terms but then had to leave because he couldn't pay his way any more. Other alumni are James Smithson (he of the Smithsonian Institute), Patrick Campbell and Michael Heseltine. HoH: MASTER. Colours: navy, scarlet and cerise.

✓ **Worcester.** Another *in* college, regarded as 'poor but dashing' by at least one LMH girl interviewed. Hearties tend to throw you into the lake. Alumni: Thomas de Quincey (who hated the place), Richard Adams and, believe it or not, Rupert Murdoch. HoH: PROVOST. Colours: pink and black.

Hertford. Pronounced *Heart-ford*; don't let anyone tell you different. A confusing college. First it was called Hart (or Hertford) Hall. As such it lasted from 1283 to 1740, when it became a college. But it was dissolved in 1805 and became Magdalen Hall (nothing, of course, to do with Magdalen, or even Magdalene, College). In 1874 it was refounded as Hertford College. Barings the bankers stumped up for the re-endowment, and there have been several recent attempts to get in on the old Founder's kin ticket. It boasts rather a puny 'Bridge of Sighs', and it starred in the tv version of *Brideshead Revisited*. Evelyn Waugh was an alumnus, not surprisingly, as was John Donne (at Hart Hall) (or Hertford). HoH: PRINCIPAL. Colours: red, maroon and white.

✗✗Keble. John Butterfield's hideous South Ken polychrome brick pile horrified Ruskin, and it will horrify you too, unless you are an ardent admirer of Betjemaniacal Victoriana at its heaviest and worst. The college owns Holman Hunt's *The Light of the World*, and it also has a new (1976) block with a space-age bar. Despite an attractive sunken lawn in its front quad (built 'to contain the inmates when rioting'), and a dinosaur (is it a stegosaurus? or a dimetrodon?) painted on the outside of its back wall (it's been there since 1971 and is freshened up every so often), this college is a haunt of hearties and gnomes, and it's out of town, and it's therefore *out*. Alumni: Chad Varah, Sir Peter Pears, Joseph Cooper. HoH: WARDEN. Colours: navy, scarlet and white.

St Edmund Hall [*sic*] is called Teddy Hall locally, and used to be so sporting that entry was granted according to your ability to catch a rugby ball (cp. Fitzwilliam, Cambridge). Ruggerbuggers still abound, though the college's most famous alumnus, Sir Robin Day, is not one, despite his shoulders. Note that the place is called a *Hall*. That is because it is the only surviving ancient Hall of the university. These were the institutions that preceded colleges. On the other hand, there are other 'halls' at Oxford, which may also be *colleges*; but not to be confused with this kind (which is, of course, now a college). HoH: PRINCIPAL. Colours: maroon and purple.

Lady Margaret Hall. Founded as the first women's college in 1878, and named after Margaret Beaufort, who, not content with being Henry VII's mother, founded John's and Christ's at Cambridge. 'LMH', as it is known, used to field, by common consent, the most sexually desirable women undergraduates, but it's now a mixed college and even has a male Principal. Waspish tongues have suggested that the first year of male intake was exclusively Gay, but whatever the truth of that it would certainly be *out* for a man to claim LMH as his college: older Oxbrites in the World Outside would only be confused and upset. For women it's probably the best one to claim to have been to, though Somerville runs a close second. Alumnae: Antonia Fraser, Dame Josephine Barnes. HoH: Principal. Colours: navy, gold and white.

✓ **Somerville, St Hugh's** and **St Hilda's** are all still all-female colleges, and now that sexually integrated colleges are proving a disaster, are likely to remain so. Recently, Somerville's First VIII has been Head of the River in the Women's Division, and the place has a good drama club too. Alumnae: Margaret Thatcher, Shirley Williams, Iris Murdoch, Dorothy L. Sayers. HoH: Principal. Colours: scarlet and black. **St Hugh's** has a toughminded pro-separatist Principal, but otherwise is very sociable. Barbara Castle went there. HoH: Principal. Colours: navy, blue, gold and white. **St Hilda's** has beautiful grounds and is just across the river from Magdalen. Dame Helen Gardner went there. HoH: Principal. Colours: navy and white.

✗ ✗ **St Anne's** was the other women's college to go mixed, with Lady Margaret Hall. Like all the colleges originally founded for women, it is well away from the centre of town, and is thus essentially *out*. Alumnae: Libby Purves, Bridget Rose Dugdale, Baroness Young. HoH: Principal. Colours: red and silver-grey.

✗ ✗ **St Peter's Hall** and **St Catherine's College** complete the main list. Each has a Master as HoH. St Peter's colours are green and gold; St Catherine's are maroon and light blue. 'Catz' (or 'Cat's'), as it is known, should not be confused with the Cambridge 'Cat's' (or 'Catz'), which is spelt **St Catharine's**. The Oxford Catz is an ultra-modern pile designed by a Dane on the edge of town.

Cambridge Colleges in Order of Foundation

The better Cambridge colleges are strung out along the *Backs* (= on the river). Cambridge colleges nearly all have Masters as HoH, so assume that to be the case unless otherwise stated. They've all gone mixed too, except for Magdalene (men), Newnham and New Hall (women). And my spies tell me that Newnham is considering going over ...

✗✗ **Peterhouse** is the oldest and traditionally one of the nastiest Cambridge colleges, and it is *never* called Peterhouse College. Its arrogance is almost as legendary as its reputation for being reactionary. It went mixed in 1985, an action remarked upon by one of its dons as 'letting the scrubbers in'. Definitely *out*, despite promising alumni, Richard Baker and James Mason. Colours: blue and white. Food and bar: grim.

✓✓ **Clare:** founded by a woman, Elizabeth de Clare, in 1326, it was one of the first to go mixed. Its Old Court and its gardens are among the most beautiful in the university, and it's popular too, so it's *in*, but consequently hard to get in*to*. Claim it if you're a liberal progressive, with an arts bias. Not only is it co-residential, but cohabitational (optional), but play this aspect down in conversation with older Oxbrites of a nervous disposition. The bridge is the oldest, and carries 14 stone balls – well, not quite. The second on the right as you approach Old Court across the river has a one-eighth slice cut out of its river-facing side; the deed was done at night by an undergraduate two hundred years ago who wanted to win a bet with a friend about the precise number of balls on the bridge. When the

the deed was done at night

bridge was renovated in the late sixties tradition was maintained, and a slice cut out of the replacement ball by the masons. This slice is now in the author's collection. *In.* Good food and college bar in the crypt. Alumnus: Hugh Latimer. Colours: black and gold. *Backs.*

✓ **Pembroke:** founded in memory of her husband (killed on her wedding day) by Mary de St Paul in 1347, it is fondly remembered by old alumni, but retains a pretty stiff public-school backbone, and therefore by modern progressive standards must be considered *borderline*. A good jumping-off point for the City or managing the family estates. Alumni: Peter Cook, William Pitt the Younger. Colours: dark blue and light blue. Food and bar: grim. (Recently, a developing interest in theatre, rock, drugs and bisexuality has tended to make Pembroke *in*.)

Gonville and Caius. Not a double-act. Gonville lived 200 years before Dr Caius refounded the place in 1557. His name is pronounced 'Keys', by the way, and the college is usually called just that. It used to be heavy on scientists, and nowadays it's pretty well known for musicians, but its reputation for *greyness* leaves it on the *borderline*. Alumni include David Frost and Titus Oates. Colours: blue and black. Food: grim. Bar: good.

Trinity Hall, known as 'Tit Hall', was founded in 1350. It used to be undistinguished but 35-year-old-plus Oxbrites retain fond memories of its bar. In these rougher times it boasts the most profitable Durex machine in the university. Alumni: Gabriel Harvey, Bulwer-Lytton, Sir Geoffrey Howe and, on the minus side, Donald McClean. Colours: black and white. Food: grim to good, depending on which Hall. *Backs*.

Corpus Christi. The interesting thing about this one is that it was founded by 'Townies'. It's small and has an attractive and very old Old Court, and the inmates are a mixture of reactionaries and liberals. It's good to have been to a college with such an impressive name, which is usually shortened to 'Corpus'. Good alumni, too, with Christopher Marlowe and Christopher Isherwood heading the field. Food and bar: bearable. Colours: cerise and white.

✓✓**King's** is really a five-star college. Once a haunt of Etonians – Etonians only, indeed, until 1861 – since 1968 it has developed a left-wing tendency which is extreme in proportion to the weight of the silver spoons King's lefties had in their mouths when they were born. King's is famous for its Chapel, whose East End was vandalized by the fellows about twenty years ago when they installed a mediocre *Adoration of the Magi* by Rubens as their altarpiece. It is also famous for its orange and green sixties bar, which rose from the ashes of a suite of Georgian rooms. The famous Carol Service was started in 1918 by Eric Milner-White. The upper-class inmates cohabit uneasily nowadays with a growing proportion of provincial scientists, but to older, influential Oxbrites in the World Outside, King's is still a name to conjure with. Dozens of famous alumni, including Rupert Brooke, E. M. Forster ('Morgan' to his friends), J. M. Keynes and, recently, Salman Rushdie. Colours, rather a disappointment after all that, mauve and white. HoH: Provost. Food: generally good. Bar: if you like that kind of thing. *Backs*.

✓**Queens'** (*note the apostrophe*) is named for Henry VI's wife and Edward IV's wife. It's popular, and the older bits are as pretty as the newer ones aren't. Erasmus was here for four years, and loved the girls but hated the beer – 'raw, small and windy'. The Anchor pub opposite keeps Queens' people lubricated these days. A cautiously *in* college. Alumni: John Fisher, T. H. White. Colours: dark green and white. HoH: President. Food and bar: bearable. *Backs*.

✗ **St Catharine's** (*note spelling*), known as 'Cat's' (or 'Catz' to younger Oxbrites) has always had a reputation for being dauntingly reactionary, but Sir Peter Hall and Howard Brenton and James Shirley were there, so It Can

Be Done From Catz, at any rate In The Theatre. One word of warning, however: the Theatre these days isn't as pro-Oxbridge as it was twenty years ago. Colours, appallingly enough, maroon and pink. Food and bar: bearable.

✓Jesus is built on the site of St Radegund's convent. 'Earlier this millennium,' said its praelector (a geologist) once, 'this college existed in another sex.' Jesus has been strong on sport, especially rowing, and its boaties have been known as a real danger to the unfair sex. It was founded in 1496 by John Alcock, who put his rebus – a cock on a ball – everywhere. Nowadays it is mixed, and Prince Edward got in (on grade 'E' passes at 'A' level, but then he's Royal), which means that any deb or Sloane with more than two grammes of brain tries desperately to be Oxbridge enough to get in and have a stab at him. Alumni: Cranmer, Coleridge, Sterne and Alastair Cooke. Colours: red and black. Food and bar: good. Currently *in*.

Christ's is good for boat-crashing coxes (Peter Hobson) – as the broken bow of the 1984 Boat Race boat, hanging in the Free Press pub in Prospect Row, testifies. Also good for Snowesque battles for Masterships, this one's rather overshadowed by the modern shops which confront it. Inside it's OK, though. A lot of heavy guns among its alumni, including Milton, Darwin, C. P. Snow, Skeate and Mountbatten. Not many recently, though, and, like Jesus, a difficult college name to conjure with in conversation in the World Outside. Food: good. Bars: bad. Colours: brown and white (very dull).

✓St John's. John's is the second largest college. Founded posthumously by Lady Margaret Beaufort in 1511, it has three attractive old courts on the east side of the river which connect with some Victorian Gothic ones on the west by a Bridge of Sighs, from which undergraduates suspended a Mini in the sixties, and whence a drunken cox once fell to his death. The boat club was founded in 1825, and it's the oldest in Cambridge. LMBC members wear loud red jackets, the first of their kind to be called 'blazers'. From a challenge to Oxford by an LMBC man in 1829 grew the Boat Race. Not surprisingly, then, a boatie college, full of brawls and buffoonery, and until lately having a dangerously high proportion of engineers (the Neanderthals of Oxbridge), and People on Army Scholarships (One Worse). Its name carries sufficient clout to make it worth considering, but it is still definitely a *borderline* case. On Ascension Day the college choir ascends to the chapel roof and does a reasonable imitation of the May Morning gig to be found at Magdalen, Oxford. It is said that the college is so rich that you can walk from John's to Lincoln Cathedral without leaving its land. Alumni: Wordsworth, Castlereagh, Palmerston and Dr Jonathan Miller (latterly a good name to drop in several different circles). Food and bar: grim. Colours: maroon and gold. *Backs.*

✓✓**Magdalene.** Pronounced 'maudlin' as at Oxford, but *note the additional 'e'.* This one gets its two stars because in certain walks of life, e.g. High Office in the Tory Party, or Estate Management in Norfolk or Lincolnshire, this is the place to have been to. Magdalene probably contains more P. G. Wodehouse throwbacks than any other Oxbridge college – until as recently as the seventies they were still coming complete with short greasy black hair, Norfolk jackets, plus-fours and dubbined brogues. Land Economy is the dominating subject, beagling and foxhunting the principal recreations (when not in pursuit of giggly, guernsey-clad Sloanes for a bit of slap and tickle). Climbing in is convenient: there's a deliberate pause in the broken bottle tops along the main street wall. The pub is the Pickerel on Magdalene Street, and a little way along is a mini and downmarket version of Jackson's, run by an unspeakably oleaginous couple, which caters to the corporeal needs of Magdalene Man. Magdalene also has the distinction of being the last college to continue the habit of candlelit Hall, and it is the last college in All Oxbridge to remain stalwartly For Men Only. With Pembroke, its May Ball is as famous as it is expensive (see more, below, Chapter 12: Balls, Parties and Sex). Alumni: Samuel Pepys, Francis Pym, Bamber Gascoigne, Charles Kingsley. Food: excellent. Bar: improving. Colours: navy and lilac. *Backs*.

✓✓ **Trinity** is Henry VIII's Cambridge foundation. It is the largest college, as Christ Church is at Oxford, and Trinity men would say that it is also the poshest (though of course they wouldn't actually use that word). They also like to think of England as having three real universities: Oxford, Cambridge and Trinity. In fact Trinity has won two more Nobel prizes than France, and three more than Italy, so why this country isn't great any more, God alone knows. The Great Court race that figured in that appallingly inaccurate film, *Chariots of Fire*, is still run, though now only by drunken Trinity beaglers who totter about in all directions being pelted with bags of flour. Trinity has had a strong public school intake in the past, but is adapting well, and with less self-consciousness than King's, to the increasing numbers of women and ordinary schoolboys flooding in these days. It has a famous boat club, called the First and Third, and an apple tree grown from a pip from alumnus Isaac Newton's famous Gravity Apple. Food is improving and central heating has now reached all rooms. Its irregular Great Court is the best in Cambridge and the biggest in Oxbridge. A list of famous alumni would take a book in itself, but the most obvious one is Lord Byron. He said of the place (in 1805) '. . . this place is the Devil, or at least his principal residence, they call it the University, but any other appellation would have suited it much better, for study is the last pursuit of the Society; the Master eats, drinks, and Sleeps, the Fellows *drink*, *dispute*, and pun, the *employments* of the under Graduates you will probably conjecture without my description . . .' *Plus ça change*, but take into account that Cambridge for Byron was Second Choice: there was no room for him at Christ Church at the time. Other recently famous alumni are: Kim Philby, Guy Burgess and Anthony Blunt, and of course the Prince of Wales. Earlier came Francis Bacon, Andrew Marvell, John Dryden, Bertrand Russell, Wittgenstein and many, many more. Tennyson's friend Arthur Hallam was here, too (so was Tennyson). Hallam called Cambridge, 'this college-studded marsh'. Colours: dark blue, with red and yellow. *Backs*.

✓ **Emmanuel,** known as 'Emma', is chiefly famous for its ducks, and its recent unilateral abolition of the Cambridge Common Entrance examination has elevated it to a King's-like status. Alumni include F. R. Leavis, Fred Hoyle, John Harvard (he of the university) and Graham Chapman – so it can't be as dull as it sounds, and it does *look* very pretty, though undesirably situated in the Main Shopping Drag. Food: good. Bar: fair. Colours: navy and pink.

✓ **Sidney Sussex.** Another one founded by a lady – Lady Frances Sidney, in 1596. Its inmates are strong on fundraising, and have topped the Rag Table for many years. Unfortunately, the noble art of raising money for charity through the Rag is generally regarded as an activity fit only for plonkers. Despite this, and despite the Roman cement which Sir Jeffry Wyatville poured all over the buildings in the 1820s in an attempt to gothickize them on the cheap, this college is slowly developing a reputation for being *in*! And this despite the threatened departure of Sainsbury's-across-the-road, until recently perhaps one of Sidney's chiefest claims to fame. Alumni: Oliver Cromwell, David Owen. Food and bar: poor. Colours: dark blue and magenta.

Downing: This one is good on rowing and science. Pretty neo-classical buildings do little else, however, to redeem it. Alumni: C. M. Doughty, John Cleese. Food: poor (Hall is the last Cambridge haven of 'sconcing' – see Chapter 8: Customs). Bar: poor. Colours: black and magenta.

Fitzwilliam is known as 'Fitz'. Only fully affiliated since 1966, this unpleasant piece of modern architecture with its cramped and overlooked rooms and its reputation for sport and general dimness is one to avoid, although its proximity to New Hall was considered a plus in the good old days of 'one college – one sex'. Ruggerbuggers predominate, and it's said of the place, as of Teddy Hall, that entrance qualifications are decided thus: at the interview they throw a rugby ball at you; if you catch it, you're in, as a pensioner. If you can catch it and pass it back, you're in as an exhibitioner; if you can catch it and convert it, you're in as a scholar. A useful pointer to the academic pretensions of Fitz is the fact that the disco is directly underneath the library. If sport is not your bag, you could claim Fitzwilliam if you want to get on in the world of music. The Fitzwilliam Quartet started here, and the place has a good reputation for music and drama. Alumni: Derek Pringle, Humphrey Burton, Norman St John-Stevas. Food: good. Bar: grim. Colours: maroon and grey.

✓**Girton** was founded as a women's college but is now mixed (1979), and has an almost 50:50 gender split. The awful red Victorian pile boasts over three miles of corridor and sits in an ample 52 acres. In the old days the Girton women were regarded as (a) intellectual, and (b) swingers, but they also had the heftiest thighs in the university, owing to the need to cycle two miles in and two miles out of town all the time. Men, of course, rarely felt equal to cycling all the way out there and then going through the palaver of climbing in. Alumnae: Muriel Bradbrooke, Arianna Stassinopoulos. Colours: green, with red and white. Food: often excellent. Bar: dull.

✓✓ **Newnham** (*Don't confuse with Cardinal New*man *who was at Oxford*) goes in for topless sunbathing in the gardens as it is still an all-female college (except for the lucky gardeners). It would like to remain so but unless it can hold out until someone wises up to the folly of mixed colleges it may have to run with the others. Like all Oxbridge women's colleges it is inconveniently and unfairly placed (at least nowadays with mixed colleges women can enjoy better architecture and somewhere central to live) and is in fact another redbrick Victorian pile. Alumnae: Margaret Drabble, Germaine Greer, Sylvia Plath and Eleanor Bron. Food: good. Bar: poor. Colours: grey, with navy and gold.

✗✗**Selwyn.** A dismal college, far out on a limb, originally helpful to the sons of poor clergymen. Don't claim this one, even if you're headed for an ecclesiastical career. Poor old Selwyn, though. It's not its fault. Strong on music. Alumni: Barry Norman, Malcolm Muggeridge. Food: poor. Bar: improving. Colours: maroon and gold.

✓**New Hall.** Founded in 1954, this is the newest all-female college. It was popular with the blokes in the sixties, and convenient for climbing in because of its notional walls and ground-floor bedrooms (inconvenient, of course, for the occupants of those rooms, which were used as passages). Rooms are cell-like, and split-level rooms for sharing are cramped and unimaginative. A famous prank was the footprints that appeared across New Hall dome mysteriously one night in the early sixties. Not bad thighs on the women, as the cycling distance from town is less than half that for Girtonians. No alumnae to speak of yet. Food and bar: bearable. Colours: navy with red, yellow and blue.

✗ ✗ Churchill. Founded as a tribute to Sir Winston in 1960, it's built to double as a conference centre in the vacs, and is thus ugly and functional. Its statutes decree that 70 per cent of its undergraduates be scientists, so avoid it if you're not one – although the 30 per cent arts people do tend to survive the blandishments of .the 'parka and woolly hat' brigade. It shares a daunting distance from town with Fitz and New Hall. Despite the liberalizing influence of the dons, it's heartening to see a number of ludicrous and reactionary drinking societies growing up at Churchill, in the best Oxbridge tradition – which only goes to show that however much you give people a chapel which is non-specifically religious, and a 'chaplain' who's a Bhagwan, the essential Englishness of Oxbridge will out. No alumni yet. Food and bar: good. Colours: chocolate and pink (rather nice).

✓ Robinson was founded in 1977 by a townie who made a fortune in the car and tv trades. Its architecture is modern-ghastly with the added eccentricity of being modelled on a mediaeval castle, complete with a blue portcullis. The place has been built to double as a conference centre, but it's also the first college *founded* as a mixed college, which is probably why none of the rooms has any privacy at all. It's far away behind the UL (the University Library, one of the most gloriously ugly buildings in England, built 1931–4 by Sir Giles Gilbert Scott) and tends to be introspective, but it's well equipped and surprisingly popular, perhaps because of a £1.8 million endowment – just for starters. Mr Robinson has spared no expense, and the college comes complete with a theatre, and a chapel with glass by John Piper and an organ by Frobenius. Undergraduates were first admitted in 1979, and I am pleased to report that degenerate drinking societies have already been formed, like lichen on stones, so that the spectres of modernization and improvement may be kept at bay for a while longer.

This completes the crucial tour of the principal colleges. Colleges are complicated but necessary to an understanding of Oxbridge, which alone among the great mediaeval foundations has retained its college system. No one knows why, say, Paris and Bologna didn't. I suspect that the colleges of the English universities simply succeeded in getting richer quicker and staying that way, thereby retaining autonomy of the university, while remaining a part of it. From these guidelines you should now be able to determine which university to claim as your own, and which college. Remember that, in general, the older, richer and central colleges are the best bet, and that while Oxford has greater historical cachet, Cambridge is far more beautiful, and is currently Favoured by Royalty. No prizes for guessing where the Princes William and Henry will be bound in a few years' time.

[3]

Town versus Gown

Oxford has a lot of facilities for townspeople, including a shop in the Covered Market where they can buy massive Doc Marten's boots especially designed for gradbashing; but facilities for undergraduates are greater and better. In Cambridge the polarization between town and gown is even more extreme.

Oxbrites enjoy college bars and discos, have parties and Balls, go punting and effectively 'own' many restaurants, pubs and shops, which cater specially to them. This is nothing new. The colleges own a lot of the towns (in fact colleges own a lot of property all over Britain in the most unlikely places, from Soho to the Highlands), and make themselves even richer by periodic dabbling in development and rent-raising. Only recently has the splendid tradition of keeping the townies in their place shown signs of weakening, with the rise of the liberal conscience, but townie disco crashing at John's and Trinity, Cambridge, in 1983 provided several patients for Addenbrooke's (the city hospital), caused the party rooms to be closed down, and left a college porter permanently deafened.

The year 1984 was rich in mugging, and the honourable if unorganized sport of gradbashing finds its annual peak at the end of the academic year, when the sight of all that *jeunesse dorée* swanning around in djs, ball gowns and punts, drinking too much and generally having a good time, gets to be too much for townie youth to bear. In Cambridge, it's the Grafton Centre vs. Trinity Street; the Bath Hotel vs. the Eagle. In Oxford few undergraduates

35

ever penetrate New Marston or Cowley, and townies shop on the Corn, but not in the Broad.

Over the years, the Oxbridge Vice-Chancellors have lost their local powers over everything from the sale of eggs to prostitution (the tarts have priced themselves out of Oxbrites' pockets these days, anyway); and the universities no longer send MPs (two each) to Westminster. These retrenchments have, however, done little to ease the traditional tension which is such a healthy feature of Oxbridge life. Like everything Oxbridge, mistrust between town and gown is firmly rooted in history; but the fighting that occasionally breaks out even today is nothing to what it was once.

The first really splendid town/gown battle got started on St Scholastica's Day, 1354, at the Swyndlestock Tavern, Oxford. Some students turned up and ordered wine, but didn't like the taste of it, and (another great Oxbridge tradition[1]) abused the landlord vigorously. Unfortunately this got his back up, and as he had some townie friends in the pub at the time, he didn't fawn and cringe as he should have done. A fight started and quickly and refreshingly escalated. Each side armed themselves with bows and arrows, and the next day the townies swarmed through the city yelling intemperate things like, 'Slea, Slea ... Havock, Havock ... Smyt fast, give gode knocks ...' A number of undergraduates were dragged from their Halls and killed, but when it was all over the Town was most severely punished, and forced to attend an annual penitential service at St Mary's (the university church) for the next 500 years.

The first endowment of Oxford University was an annual fine imposed on the town for hanging a clerk in 1209.

---

[1] *Always treat townie tradesmen like dirt.* Some, described collectively as 'Oxbridge sniveldom', actively enjoy it.

'*Slea, Slea . . . Havock, Havock . . .*'

Originally worth £1.60, it has increased with inflation to £3.08 today, and still forms part of the Vice-Chancellor's fund for Needy Scholars. And for over 600 years, every Oxford graduand was required to swear, on taking his degree, that he'd never be reconciled with someone called Henry the son of Simeon, who murdered a Fellow in 1242.

In Cambridge in 1380 a mob sacked Corpus for betraying its townie origins. Mass at Great St Mary's (the university church) was interrupted, and university muniments were burnt. The Mayor and bailiffs forced the Masters and scholars to sign deeds renouncing all the privileges granted to them by the king, and promising to conform to the town and borough laws. Sadly, this splendid act of righteous indignation was quickly squashed by the Establishment in the form of the Bishop of Norwich, who promptly moved in with some soldiers, had the new deeds revoked and hanged a few townies for good measure.

On the other hand, in 1908 an undergraduate beat up a Cambridge policeman so badly that the man was permanently crippled and had to retire from the force. In those days the university courts still had jurisdiction over student pranks of this sort, in a discretionary way, and the undergraduate was let off with a stern warning – on condition, of course, that he *never did it again*.

Rumbles of town and gown can be fun: the author remembers a fantastic punt battle (a gown punt versus a town punt) that took place quite spontaneously on the Cam, where water splashed with paddles was all that was thrown. Both punts sank, a lot of tourists were distressed, and everyone was soaked, but laughing. One very rare instance of friendly contact being made.

Contact of another kind is that between town and gown on the field of love (or, more correctly, sex). A distinction you must learn is that whereas at Oxford it's perfectly OK – and even preferable – for male undergraduates to go out with town women, at Cambridge not only is this practice rarely taken up, it is looked down on and deplored. And no female Oxbrite ever goes out with a townie male. That really would be the Beginning of the End!

None of this, of course, applies to Gay Oxbrites, although the tendency for them is to carry on gently within the confines of their own college. Ambitious Cambridge Gays should claim to be King's men (or women).

More on all this at a more appropriate moment, later on (Chapter 12: Social Life II).

【4】

Arrival – getting up and what to
do then

NOTE FIRST OF ALL that you 'go up' to Oxbridge. You do
this at the beginning of every term and at the end of it you
'go down'. 'How long have you been down for?' or 'How
long are you going to be down?' are not inquiries about
depression, in Oxbridgese. At the end of your course, i.e.
after three or four years, you 'come down' for good. 'She
went down in 1975' doesn't mean she died then. There's
an important distinction, too, between 'went down' and
'sent down'. 'Sent down' means expelled, and you have to
be a pretty tough cookie for that to happen to you these
days. It's almost as hard as getting sacked from the BBC.
Depending on circumstances, though, being sent down
can carry a lot of kudos in later life. 'He was sent down for
burning his papers in Schools/the Senate House' isn't bad.
Debagging a proctor *sounds* fine, but as it's rather *passé* it
should only be used by older Oxbrites. You wouldn't be
sent down for that these days anyway. Rustication is a
variant: it means you're kicked out for a while to cool off,
but then you can come back if you want to, and are
suitably penitent.

Before any of this happens, however, you have to Get
In.

Getting In depends on a lot of things. It used to be good
grades at 'A' level, followed by passing your college
entrance examinations and an interview. Nowadays it
might just be by interview, if you're both lucky and a
brilliant bluffer. The Cambridge university general

entrance exam, known as a 'Previous', and nicknamed 'Little Go', disappeared twenty years ago. Oxford had a similar thing, only it was called 'Responsions'. (Of course, Oxford also had a thing called 'littlego', but it was the same level of exam as 'Mods'. And while we are on the subject, 'Greats' is the second and final part of the classical honours course.) Passing 'Little Go' only meant that you had the minimum entry requirement for entering the university, *but* any individual college could set you a further, harder exam of its own. The university is just a federation of autonomous and fiercely independent colleges; this is the single most confusing thing about Oxbridge, and it has to be learned. In 1931 Oxford rather helplessly (or possibly cannily, since it was in response to an Enquiry From Outside – never welcomed by Oxbridge) said that 'there is no person or body in Oxford, competent or qualified to declare what the functions of the university are'.

It gets worse: if you pass a Scholarship examination, you become a Scholar. This may mean a special gown (see more in Chapter 10: Dress Sense) and about £100 a year. If you don't quite make that, but you're better than a pleb, you can be an Exhibitioner (*c*. £60 a year). Ordinary Oxbrites are called Commoners at Oxford and, even more disparagingly, Pensioners at Cambridge. Be grateful. It used to be even more complicated.

Exams are fine, they are pretty well like ultra-tough 'A' levels, though beware of Oxbridge quirkiness. Someone once attempting a scholarship exam in English was confronted by the question, 'Show by a comparison of their styles why you think Blake and Jane Austen were writing at the same time'. He foolishly attempted this trap question and ended up as a mere Pensioner.

Much more worrying than exams, though, are *Interviews*.

Oxford and Cambridge both have foul weather

(Cambridge is fond of telling you that there's nothing to protect the town from the East Winds until the Urals), and interviews are generally conducted around November to give the frost and the fog the best opportunities of biting and intimidating the would-be Oxbrite. You are summoned to a bewildering old building (a college), and when you finally decipher the various notices that tell you where you've got to be when (unless you're lucky enough to be trying for a liberal college which will have told you in a letter), you find yourself in an antique den with (usually) very masculine décor, confronted by one or more apparently demented, or bored, middle-aged men in tweed jackets. Nowadays, you may get the even more terrifying female equivalent of this.

There are many stories about interviews, and most of them are apocryphal: be armed against them. Two general rules may be inferred from the stories, however: (a) they have probably made up their minds about you already; (b) few interviews have anything to do with the subject you want to read. The following true case histories will give you some idea of what happens. Names have been changed to protect the innocent.

'Scottie', interviewed to read History at Trinity, Cambridge: at his interview he was asked if he had ever written any poetry (he had) and could he recite some (he couldn't). He was given tea in a cup which leaked so fast into the saucer that it overflowed and soaked his trousers, scalding him. At this juncture the interviewing don leant too far backwards in his seat and crashed into a glass bookcase behind him. 'Scottie' was accepted.

'Aloysius', interviewed to read History at Oriel: at his interview he found two dons who, having discovered that he came from Liverpool, asked him what horse he fancied for the Grand National. As this was in November, 'Aloysius' had no idea who was even running at Aintree, but he gave the name of a horse he knew of. He was accepted.

'Morgan', interviewed to read Classics at Magdalene. Asked what he thought about student unrest, he shrewdly replied, 'Oh, it's all to do with these Communist agitators' – and got in.

Getting In depends on your school too. Though public school is less important these days, it helps to have been to one of the better known ones. 'Aloysius' came from a grammar school which had never sent anyone to Oxbridge before. His schoolmasters hadn't got a clue. They plumped for Oxford because of the Dictionary, and advised him to try for Oriel because it was the only college none of them had heard of – concluding from this that it must be so obscure that with the attendant diminished competition he would have a better chance of getting in there.

Once the hurdles of Getting In are jumped, and he or she is accepted, the Oxbrite Goes Up – generally early in October. At Cambridge, that's it. At Oxford, you have to don *subfusc* (see Chapter 10: Dress Sense) and Matriculate at the Sheldonian Theatre. There is nothing to be afraid of: no one asks any awkward questions. You just mill around in your gown, grasping your cap, and have the Vice-Chancellor drone at you in Latin. You won't see him again until you graduate.

Three tasks now await you.

The first is pretty well decided for you. If you have chosen your college carefully, it will provide you with rooms for your first year. These may be Nice, or Grotty. The richer (and older) the college, the nicer the rooms. The Importance Of Nice Rooms to fledgling Oxbrites (or 'freshmen' abbr. 'freshers' – as they are called) cannot be exaggerated. They may decide their social life for them. Most get a bedsit. The really lucky ones get a sitting room with a bedroom *en suite*. If you are in a liberal/co-residential college, *Do Not Cohabit Immediately*. You will regret it, and if you are not careful you will find yourself pinioned: you do not want to go through a dress-rehearsal for a divorce at this stage. The Real Thing will come soon enough in the World Outside. For this reason too, avoid freshers' 'hops' and discos – they are meat markets whose main purpose is to allow second and third-year men to have a look at the new intake of female talent. Male freshers won't stand a chance of scoring, unless they fall victim to a predatory second or third-year woman undergraduate.

The second task is Transport. Only under exceptional circumstances will you be allowed to run a car, because the traffic is so congested anyway, especially in Cambridge. Some Oxbrites cheat, and keep one unofficially. Car-sharing isn't uncommon, but in such cases the car must be a Battered Heap. (Old VWs are popular, but beware. One King's man borrowed a friend's VW to go to Oxford for the weekend. On his return, the friend asked him why he hadn't borrowed the car after all. He had in fact taken *another* VW, identical in all but number plate, and simply hadn't noticed; and its owner couldn't report its loss because it was 'unofficial'.) Sports cars are the preserve of the very rich, who live outside town in houses Daddy and Mummie have bought them, and commute in for lectures. In the late sixties there was one red MGB at Cambridge, owned by a Hong Kong Chinese: it was the only sports car in undergraduate circles, and oddly, it didn't help him pull any more girls than anyone else – well, not much.

Motorbikes and mopeds have their charms, and have the advantage with cars of getting you out to restaurants and pubs in the surrounding countryside, but the standard Oxbrite form of transport is still the Bicycle. Avoid tandems for the same reasons that you avoid cohabitation. Townie drivers will loathe you because you

Avoid tandems

will ride with reckless abandon. Oxbrites in later life reminisce vaguely and affectionately about cycling, but most never do it again, and for some reason cycling anecdotes are the immediate mark of a Bore, and are thus to be avoided. However, the keen Oxbrite will know that bicycles were first introduced to Cambridge from Paris in 1869. Lord Dunedin was the first undergraduate to ride one. Cycling races had been started between the two universities by 1874, and in 1903, fining a man 5*s.* for reckless cycling at Sheep's Green, a local Cambridge magistrate said, 'There is scarcely a place in Cambridge now where pedestrians can walk with safety. Cyclists are an utterly reckless class, who don't care tuppence about other people. They are the most selfish people in the world.'

The best time to buy a bike is at the beginning of the Michaelmas term at one of the police auctions or Annual Sales. Clever Oxbrites get theirs registered with the police, or at least painted with the college 'letter' and an individual number, to avoid theft.

The third task is the most important. It is called Establishing Yourself. Oxbrites reminisce about this a lot. You will find that most were at first daunted by the array of scintillating intelligences they suddenly found themselves surrounded by. Some will more honestly tell you that they were not. If in doubt, be noncommittal: all Oxbrites are incredibly garrulous and will plough on regardless, to tell you of how they managed to Establish Themselves.

If you came from a school that sends a lot of people to Oxbridge, you will find yourself surrounded by instant society; but never forget that *All Oxbrites Spend the Second Two Years Avoiding the Friends They Made in the First Year.* This is profoundly true. The thing to remember is that you are not alone: all freshers are at sea, jostling and jockeying for position in an attempt to keep their peckers up. The cockiest and most confident bloke within earshot is probably miserably homesick underneath.

Within a week of Going Up new Oxbrites are deluged with invitations. These will panic them. At Oxford they will go to the Freshmen's Fair; at Cambridge to the Societies' Fair. Here, in a babel that makes the Futures Market look like a religious retreat, they will be confronted with the booths of hundreds of clubs to join. More on this later. For the moment, take the point that there is no lack of opportunity. The subtle problem is still to be overcome, though; because Establishing Yourself really means In The Eyes Of Others. The solution is easy: you must look as if you owned the place. Confidence is all. This is why in later life Oxbrites tend to go around brazening everything out. As it has always been, and still is, tougher on women, you will find that female Oxbrites get on well in tv production and publishing, thanks to the techniques of survival they learned at their Alma Mater. A helpful practical hint is to arm yourself immediately with a *Varsity Handbook* (Cambridge), an *Oxford Handbook*, *Cherwell Handbook* and a *Vade Mecum* (Oxford). These books warn the fledgling Oxbrite what to expect. Oxbridge nowadays even provides a *Little Blue Book*, which is a guide to sex for those new to it.

Two specific examples of self-establishment follow:

'Antonia' arrived at Clare College to read English. She was paired for supervisions (see Chapter 5: Vita Academica) with someone who, at 19, was already an established poet and Gregory Award winner. This sensitive soul (fingers constantly twisting and untwisting in an ecstasy of artistic sensibility) saw fit to snigger derisively when 'Antonia' read out her essays on, for example, Julian of Norwich. The other six Clare English freshers were pretty daunting, too, and 'Antonia' felt that conversation was in danger of slipping away from her entirely. Desperation gave her a plan. In conversation one night in Hall, she casually dropped the name of Andrei Czernowski, a Polish novelist of the late nineteenth century who had only been translated into French, but who had had a profound influence on Ibsen and Shaw. She cited one novel in particular, *Qu'il pleuve*. There was a nervous silence. Then her fellow freshers started to 'remember' all about Czernowski, argued with her about

Qu'il pleuve, and even mentioned the titles of some of his other novels. This reaction relieved 'Antonia' greatly, since Czernowski didn't exist: she had just invented him. Nobody, you will notice, paused to wonder whether Ibsen or Shaw read Polish or French well enough to *be* influenced by Czernowski. They were all so anxious not to be thought ignorant that they just plunged in and bullshitted. The ability to do this is one of the principal marks of the Oxbrite. To say, 'I've never heard of it', or 'I don't understand' is always considered *infra dig*. Realizing that everyone was as panicky as she was, 'Antonia' Established Herself, rejected the lot of them (especially the one with greasy black hair who went in for the pawing technique), and went on to become a leading lady in Footlights, and President of the ADC.

'O'Flaherty' came from a grammar school in Liverpool to Christ Church in the mid-sixties. He did admittedly have curiosity value in that college at that time, and a certain reflected glory was his too, on account of the Beatles coming from Liverpool.

This was at the time when Happenings were fashionable, and in order to establish himself, 'O'Flaherty' decided to have one in his rooms. He went to a butcher and bought a sheep's eye. This he embedded in sand in a small cardboard pill box and then wrapped it up as for a game of Pass-the-Parcel. His guests arrived in his rooms, and drank beer (a novelty for the upper-class Oxbrites among them). He had taken care to invite a cross-section: tall blond men from the Home Counties, and little dark ones from Halifax and worse. When everyone was sufficiently lubricated, the Happening began, and the parcel was passed. The 'victim' was an old Etonian who opened the box, brayed in horror (and mistakenly), 'Oh my God, it's a prick!', and fainted. 'O'Flaherty' thus secured a reputation for being a bit of a dangerous character, and enjoyed huge success from then on.

Pseuds of course will go to quite unnatural lengths to establish themselves. One bought a shelf-load of Penguin Classics, and proceeded methodically to bend back their black spines so that they cracked and the white cardboard beneath showed through – to make it look as if he'd read them – see more, below, Chapter 11: Social Life I.

〔5〕

Vita Academica[1]

THIS CANNOT be ignored. Gone are the days when King's men were exempt from all exams and just took degrees anyway, or when in the late eighteenth century Lord Eldon, doing Schools in Hebrew and History, was simply asked, 'What is the Hebrew for "The place of the skull", and who founded University College?': 'Golgotha, and Alfred the Great,' said Lord Eldon. 'Congratulations,' said the examiner.

Life is tougher now, and it is a sign of the times that *work*, even among non-scientists, is *in*.

First of all, the Oxbrite (unless he is a scientist) is left to fend for himself a lot. Most Humanities do not have obligatory lectures, and a typical Oxbrite will go to six or seven near the beginning of his first year, a couple (owing to guilty conscience) in his second, and none thereafter, having learnt the lesson that reading the lecturer's book on the subject is both quicker and more convenient. It has been scurrilously suggested that some dons deliberately give bad lectures, in order to drive people to buy their books. Whatever the truth of that, I am convinced that there is none in the story of the lecturer who brought a couple of dozen copies of his latest work to a lecture to sell to the undergraduates. There is a rule that dons need not lecture if fewer than two people are present. When women were first gaining a foothold, one old Fellow was confronted by just one male and one female undergraduate in his lecture room. Addressing the man, he said, 'Sir,

[1] See also Chapter 10: Dress Sense.

since you are the only person present, I shall not lecture today.'

So much for lectures. The cornerstone of being taught is the supervision, at Cambridge, which is an hour's meeting once a week with your supervisor, a don specializing in a particular branch of your subject. You generally go in pairs, and take it in turn to read out an essay and have one marked. This is generally unnerving. It's hard to pull the wool over a supervisor's eyes – though on one memorable occasion an Oxbrite entirely unnerved an inexperienced supervisor by writing a long and authoritative essay on the Restoration playwright Thomas Ipswich (who does not, of course, exist). Generally, supervisors are like coiled springs, taking special delight in destroying the entire premise of an essay with one Hard Fact. The same (roughly) goes for Oxford, except that it's called a tutorial, and the don in question is called your tutor. Your *tutor* at Cambridge is also a don, but *he's* the equivalent of your *Moral Tutor* at Oxford. And of course at Cambridge you have the additional luxury of a Director of Studies to supervise your work in general. At Oxford you have to make do with a Senior Tutor. At Cambridge, of course, the Senior Tutor may *also* be your tutor, but your *tutor* is *never* your supervisor, or even your Director of Studies, since your tutor never shares your subject.

How you are taught should now be clear. Before moving on to the more complicated question of exams (and some knowledge of the system is vital), the question of subjects should be considered. Some are *in*, others are *out*. In the following table *grey* subjects marked with an asterisk move *in* and *out* of fashion; those left unmarked remain *grey*. Remember that the more popular the subject, the harder it is to get in on. This list is representative. Nearly every conceivable subject is taught, but you cannot (yet) read Creative Accountancy, Advertising or

51

Domestic Science, as you can at most American and some
ordinary British 'universities'.

IN	GREY	OUT
Classics – Oxon.		
English	Modern languages*	Geography
PPE	Medicine*	Engineering
(Politics,		(all types)
Philosophy,		
Economics) –	History*	Anglo-Saxon
Oxon.	Sciences (all)	Education
Archaeology &		
Anthropology		
('Ark'n'Anth')	Architecture	Land
History of Art	Law*	Economy
		Social and
		Political
	Philosophy*	Sciences
	Music	Theology

Having taken note of that list, it is also worth
remembering that fashion has nothing to do with reality.
Medicine, accounting and engineering offer the best job
prospects today, and zoology and philosophy the worst.
Cutbacks in the public services, teaching and higher
education mean fewer jobs for arts graduates, although
the number of arts graduates is steadily on the increase
(see more below, Chapter 16: Life After Oxbridge).

Exams: at Cambridge the first one you get (depending on
your subject) is Prelims (= preliminary examinations).
These happen after one or two years (depending on your
subject), and although they are graded, mean little: they
are there to check your progress, and can be treated with
contempt. The heavy guns are brought out for Tripos (the
name derives from the three-legged stool upon which

mediaeval examiners apparently found it convenient to sit). These come as Part I and Part II, and are taken after two and three years (depending on subject). Part II is also Finals, so the grade you get in Part II is the grade your degree will be in. Borderline grades are determined by 'vivas' (= viva voce) – a terrifying experience in which you are grilled orally. At Oxford things are a little more complicated, and luckily most Oxford Oxbrites forget the details after a few years. They do not, however, forget the *words*, and don't count on them forgetting *anything*.

Everything depends on the subject, of course, but it's important to understand basic distinctions:

At Oxford, you usually take Mods (= Moderations, and not to be confused with Modern History) at the end of the third term. You sit about six papers, which aren't too hard, but if you fail, you're out. Or you might take Prelims, additionally or possibly alternatively, depending on the subject, but which are not at all like Cambridge Prelims. They have fewer and tougher papers than Mods, but not graded, and if you fail you can retake. These happen at the end of the second or third term. PPE Prelims are at the end of the third term, but History Mods are at the end of the first term of all. If you survive all this you can go on to Schools (= Finals, but it's also the name of the place where you sit them – the Examination Schools – which are of course not to be confused with Old Schools at Cambridge, which deal with university administration). Schools are graded and that grade is the grade of your degree.

At Oxford, where building up exam tension has been developed into a fine art, you wear full academic dress for all exams, i.e. subfusc, and you must have your cap with you, though you do not *wear* it. You only wear the thing when you matriculate and when you graduate. At Cambridge, you wear a gown for examinations, but full academic dress only for graduation. And even then you don't need a square – on your head or in your hand. For more on the vexed question of gowns, hoods, squares (caps) and so on, see Chapter 10: Dress Sense. Some Oxford Oxbrites go very vague and defensive when they are questioned on the subject of when what is worn, or held, so do not despair if you slip up – just claim to have forgotten details. At Oxford, there is no examination at the end of the second year, except for Classicists, who sit Mods at the end of their fifth term – but as they do a four-year course, their third year is exam-free.

Oxbrites always pretend to have forgotten what grade they got, or tell you that it doesn't matter any more anyway (once they are out in the World Outside), but the fact is that not only do they *never* forget, but their own grade, and the grades of their peers, remain of very keen interest to them for the rest of their lives.

It is now thought *in* to have a First (if you are under 35), although a Starred First is so rare that if you say you've got one you'll either excite the suspicion that you are lying, or that you are a freak. Neither is desirable. At Cambridge, Seconds are broken down into Upper Seconds (two-ones), and Lower Seconds (two-twos), and it looks as if Oxford will soon follow suit. Two-ones are *most* desirable, and a two-one plus the presidency of a good university society is still the best recommendation you can give yourself. Potential employers will think that you could have got a First if you hadn't decided to distinguish yourself in extra-mural activities as well. Also, people with Firsts tend to daunt Oxbrites and non-Oxbrites alike in the World Outside. A two-one indicates becoming and manageable intelligence.

Thirds have a certain cachet, so if you get saddled with one, do not despair. An Oxbrite of the author's acquaintance successfully got the job of Head of Broadcasting in a newly-rich Arab state by telling them that Thirds were top and Firsts were bottom of the grading scale. And if you can't pull that sort of stunt off, don't despair either. Gibbon, Dr Johnson, de Quincey, Swinburne and Ruskin all failed to sit their degrees; Shelley, John Locke and Sir Richard Burton were sent down; and Matthew Arnold and Cardinal Newman failed to get Firsts.

If you can't face Finals and you are resourceful, you can feign illness, and get an aegrotat, but these are undesirable as they make you seem feeble. Oxbrites with aegrotats are often driven to vaulting ambition in the World Outside to make up for them.

A final word on exams: do not fail. If you think you might, leave the University a term or two before Finals, declaring that you have had enough of this delayed adolescent existence, and you are off to Make Your Name in the World Outside. This will excite the admiration, if not the emulation, of your peers, and non-Oxbrites in positions of power will feel more comfortable with you, too. Only resort to Being Sent Down if you can find a suitably original way of doing it (you can still be sent down for shooting a deer in Magdalen Park); nothing fails more miserably than a damp squib.

If you pass, however you pass, there is one great consolation for all the complication and difficulty Oxbrites have to undergo: in a system unique to Oxbridge (and viewed with chagrin by ordinary universities); if you pass your BA, you get your MA free! Well, not *free*, but on payment of a small fee, and after a three-year wait at Cambridge (seven at Oxford). Non-Oxbrites are often fooled by MA(Oxon.), or MA(Cantab.) after a person's name: they think they should be impressed. You should capitalize on this for all it is worth. Cognoscenti, however, would probably agree with the early sixteenth-century judgement that:

> A Mayster of Arte
> Is not worth a Farte.

〖6〗

The Staff – staff problems

ANCIENT OXBRITES can remember the time when college servants were on call from dawn to dusk. They would earn next to nothing, and for it they would make up fires in the rooms in winter at 6 a.m., so that warmth would have penetrated the mediaeval walls by the time the inmates arose (at *c.* 9 a.m.); they would carry logs and coal up, and ashes down, seven flights of stairs; they would do the same with 'nightsoil' and hot water for washing. They would prepare, cook, clear away and wash up breakfast (and lunch and dinner if required), clean the rooms, polish shoes and generally be at the inmates' beck and call for any little errands. All this so that the Oxbrites whom they attended would be left free to concentrate on what they were there for (at least theoretically): the Pursuit of Wisdom. Each servant, or pair of servants, would have responsibility for a 'staircase' of rooms, containing several undergraduates. Fellows were even luckier: they might have a personal servant. As late as the sixties one bachelor Oxford don, who lived in college, had this code of communication with his servant: his rooms were *en suite*: sitting room/bathroom/bedroom. In the morning, the servant entering the sitting room knew *not* to disturb, and to leave *two* breakfasts, if the door between the bathroom and the bedroom was closed. Kitchens (called gyp rooms at Cambridge) were out in the hall, shared between two rooms or more.

In those days nearly all the servants were men, attending on men; it was an honourable profession, often handed down from father to son, and servants would be so jealous of their work that at least one liberal Oxbrite, attempting to make his own bed, was soundly berated for doing so.

As time passed, and women arrived, college servants developed a secondary and less welcome duty: because one of their jobs was to wake you up in the morning (and of course they had a key to your rooms), having a woman to stay overnight was next to impossible. It was considered the height of good fortune to get onto the staircase of a bribable servant: in 1964 £1 would secure discretion. Such bribes are no longer necessary: Oxbridge ingenuity proved too much in the end for both servants and college authorities, and by the end of the sixties the more liberal colleges were already instructing servants only to enter rooms in the mornings if not instructed to the contrary (a note pinned to the door) by the inmate. Copulation throve. On one occasion, a male Oxbrite pinned the 'Wake Me Up' note to his door by accident, instead of the 'Do Not Disturb' one. His servant duly came in, took one look at the mound in the bed, and bolted. In her absence the Oxbrite checked the note, and replaced it with the correct one. Later the servant apologized for misreading his note. Why was she so compliant? Because by lucky chance she had accidentally broken one of the Oxbrite's claret glasses right at the beginning of term. He'd had the sense to be forgiving, thus wrapping her around his little finger for good.

As we've seen, names of things and people vary from Oxford to Cambridge. For example, the square formed by the surrounding buildings of a college is usually grassed, and only Fellows may walk on this grass. The square is called a 'quad' at Oxford (= quadrangle) and a 'court' at Cambridge. The same kind of thing goes for college servants. At Oxford he or she is called a 'scout'; at Cambridge, he is called a 'gyp', and she is called a 'bedder' (= bedmaker; and the word is also used to a certain extent,

57

depending on the college, at Oxford). Bedders are nothing new; they've been around since the eighteenth century, in small numbers. Nowadays they are beginning to outnumber the men. At first bedders were chosen for their advanced years and ugliness, and they were English. The servant problem changed all this. As early as the late sixties one Jesus, Cambridge, man had a Polish bedder in his final year. She was old and ugly, but could speak virtually no English, and was also so terrified of electricity that she wouldn't even turn his electric fire on in the mornings. This meant that getting up in winter made him feel like Captain Oates. The Polish bedder heralded the end of the old, reliable, East Anglian professional servant. In the same Oxbrite's first year he had had a Suffolk lady to look after him, who could remember not only cooking and serving breakfast, lunch and dinner, but laying out clothes, too. The Polish bedders weren't all bad, though: a Clare man had a 28-year-old blonde one, and as she was bored with her stolid East Anglian husband, he enjoyed a wild affair with her for the whole of his first year – to the envy of his fellow inmates.

Servants will remember you – especially if you were a good tipper. One ex-Oriel Oxbrite, ill-advisedly returning to Oxford to take his MA in person, was approached after a freezing night in college by his old scout:

> SCOUT: It's Mizter Z—, izn't it?
> OXBRITE: Yes, Mac, it's me. (*Leaden pause.*) How are you?
> SCOUT (*With enthusiasm*): Ooh, Mizter Z—, wee're moore mizrable than everr.

Oxbrites don't usually live in college for all their three years – but servants under a different guise take the form outside of Approved Landladies. These can be kindly, or fierce or simply human. A Gay Jesus man spent his second year with a fierce landlady, but she adored him: 'Oh, Mr

S–, you're such a *good* boy. I never have any trouble with you and girls. And you always bring such nice quiet young men back with you at night.' A New College man was forced to spend his third year in digs, and had to have an Approved Landlady. Luckily the landlady was human: she had a lover (by coincidence the Head Porter at New College), and took the line that 'what the eye doesn't see . . .'; this meant that 'Dylan' could cheerfully go on sleeping with his girlfriend, although of course using the bathroom in the mornings quite often became Feydeauesque, since neither the Head Porter nor the girlfriend could be allowed to see *each other*.

Before leaving servants, a word of advice: only older (35+) Oxbrites will have real horror stories, or indeed any stories, to tell of them. Liberalism has drawn their teeth since the sixties, and nowadays they are reduced to the level of mere cleaners. But treat them as a luxury you will probably never enjoy again.

The next group of staff the Oxbrite has to deal with is porters. These men, bowler-hatted and soberly dressed, sit in a stuffy, overheated, glassfronted office (called a 'lodge') at the front of each college, and treat you with all the crocodile deference of a policeman booking you for speeding. The chief of this crew is usually a grizzled ex-NCO who never lets you forget it. Have as little to do with porters as possible – it will still be more than enough – and certainly never attempt to fraternize with them. It confuses them and can make them turn nasty. Porters used to be the people who would move from the shadows into the lamplight as you were in the middle of climbing in with a woman, and give vent to some such pellucid witticism as 'Good evening, Mr X, having a spot of bother/taking a bit of exercise, are we?', and fall then into smiling silence as you babble something about her being your sister and all the hotels in town full.

Let him have his fun. The woman will have to go home,

but all the porter can really do is report you to your tutor/moral tutor, who will be bored and tell you not to do it again. Treat porters with respect, however, or you will not only get fined but you will be thought Not A Gentleman, and life thereafter will be miserable for you. It's sometimes difficult to feel sympathy for a porter, but a moment's reflection on how little he's paid often does the trick. A St John's porter told me that in the sixties when he had taken the job he had had to sign a 22-page contract – 'practically the Official Secrets Act' – that effectively barred him from 'tattling about what went on inside'; he was paid 'lower than farm wages' for the job. His starting salary was £9 per week.

From the ranks of the porters come the Bulldogs. The author has been fortunate in running one to earth and interviewing him. Bulldogs (so called at both universities) are the university policemen. They wear black jackets and waistcoats, and black and grey striped trousers. At Oxford they wear bowlers, and at Cambridge, black top hats (but younger Oxbrites note: this is no longer so at Cambridge, except ceremonially). In the old days, when there were far more rules to break, Oxbrites could have fun eluding Bulldogs, but now their power has waned to such an extent that even a 30-year-old Oxbrite may have passed all his time 'up' without ever seeing one.

Bulldogs, hunting in pairs, attend a *Proctor*. A proctor is an academic with special policing powers. In Oxford such an officer has been on record since 1267. There are two proctors at a time, and each is attended by two Bulldogs. If caught doing something they shouldn't in the old days, Oxbrites were 'progged' – i.e. the proctor would raise his cap politely and say, 'Are you a member of this university?' (knowing full well that you were), and fine you 6s. 8d. each (the equivalent of half a mediaeval mark). For what Oxbrites had to do to deserve this, see Chapter 7: Rules. Older Oxbrites only need worry about these: like

ACADEMIC
[OLD STYLE]

ACADEMIC
[MODERN]

the Bulldog, the proctor's role has effectively dwindled to a ceremonial one.

Fellows and dons and the rest of the academic crew form the remainder of the basic staff of Oxbridge. These people would be annoyed if they were to hear themselves described as staff, because traditionally the universities exist for them to do research and drink claret in. Teaching and lecturing are disagreeable interruptions to this pleasant existence (spiced with internecine intrigue), but supper has to be sung for. Any form of discipline in existence is easily ducked out of, however, by becoming eccentric. Sadly, only the BBC, outside Oxbridge, genuinely nurtures and protects its dead wood nowadays.

All Oxbrites reminisce about dotty dons. The word 'don' comes from the Latin *dominus* (as does the Spanish title). All Fellows are dons, but not all dons are necessarily Fellows. Often Visiting Professors from foreign parts are not allowed to become either, and at Oxford they have to be given a nominal Oxford degree on top of their own ones in order to be allowed in at all. Election to a Fellowship of All Souls (and, unkind tongues would say, a sinecure for life) is election to a genial club which will keep a roof over your head and port in your belly until the day you die, as well as providing you with an army of powerful political and industrial contacts, without your having to do a thing in return (except occasionally pray for the souls of the English dead of the Hundred Years War). Of course most Fellows take life a little more seriously than that, and in liberal colleges they have to, but if you are a graduate co-opted and incorporated a member of your college, you are *in* like Flynn. If this is granted to you really early, say at 21, you may look back on your career in later life and think it was a mixed blessing; but most cling like mad, despite the cloistered existence. It is typically Oxbridge that the college servant who brings news to a graduate of election to Fellowship introduces it as 'disagreeable'. Always expect the unexpected from Oxbridge: it does have its own twisted logic, and by these little signs do Oxbrites know each other. To get into their circle you must pass muster faultlessly: but it's only a question of cracking the code.

Dons (and Fellows) work as professors, Readers, lecturers, Lay Deans, proctors, supervisors, tutors, bursars, Wine Stewards and so on. Definitions of all these are immaterial to our purposes since most Oxbrites forget which don did what within a few years of coming down. They do not, however, forget what any given don's *subject* was. Beware. If you do nothing else, learn the subjects of eccentric dons whom Oxbrites are likely to reminisce about.

You will hear of someone being referred to as a 'Persian don' or a 'Russian don'. This does not refer to their nationality, as will become apparent from 'Old Norse don', 'Anglo-Saxon don' or, more obviously still, 'History don', but to their subject. Some modern dons have written interminable novels about what it is to be a don: these are worth ploughing through on the basis of the premise, 'know your enemy'. You could make a start with C. P. Snow's *The Masters*.

Dons often find undergraduates an irritating interruption to slanging each other, though they agree that the purpose of lectures is 'less to impart knowledge, than to show off what you know'. Two dons at New College, whom we shall call Erpingham and McDonald, hadn't spoken to each other for 20 years or more. When forced to sit next to each other at High Table, they even asked for the salt to be passed via an intermediary. The reason for this unfriendliness was that when Erpingham had first joined the college, McDonald had called him, by accident or design, 'Pilkington'. Erpingham never recovered from his pique at this.

They like slanging everyone else too. Maurice Bowra[1] was good at it: 'Awful shit: never met him'; and in the eighteenth century, when dons really *were* lazy, Thomas Hearne described Sir John Vanbrugh simply as 'a blockhead', and dismissed George Frederick Handel and his orchestra as 'a lowsy crew of foreign fidlers'. Younger Oxbrites will remember the Fundamentalist versus Structuralist furore in the Cambridge English faculty in 1981. Rix vilified McCabe; McCabe hit back, with Williams leaping to his defence. But Oxbrites in the World Outside approach this subject rarely as they sit lunching together at Joe Allen's, or if it *is* introduced they shy away, or turn the conversation. They do not wish to admit that they really wouldn't know a structuralist if hit in the face with one. Or a fundamentalist, for that matter. Order another bottle and stick to more comfortable subjects – like sex (see below, Chapter 12: Social Life II).

Legendary dons are legion. A handful of the best will set you on the right path. Just for starters, reflect that Walter Pater, John Ruskin and Charles Dodgson (Lewis Carroll) were all at Oxford at about the same time. Owing to their various difficulties with sex, they earned the nicknames respectively of Wouldn't, Couldn't and Shouldn't. Others include Canon William Buckland (1784–1836), Oxford's first Professor of Geology. Visiting the shrine of St Rosalia in Sicily on his honeymoon, he instantly declared the sacred relics of the saint to be 'the bones of a goat'; the miraculous freshness of a martyr's 'blood' on the stone flags of an ancient cathedral was explained by him with equal robustness. 'It's bats' urine,' he said, having licked

[1] To Bowra is credited the following story: Bathing nude at Parsons' Pleasure with a colleague, they were interrupted by a party of schoolgirls. The colleague covered his genitals with his towel; Bowra covered his head. After the giggling throng had passed, the colleague asked Bowra the reason for his action. 'In these parts,' replied the Professor of Poetry, 'I am known by my face.'

it. He filled his house with all sorts of animals, and had experimented by eating most living things. His least favourite foods were mole, and bluebottles. He also once ate the mummified heart of a mediaeval king of France.

A less attractive Victorian don was the Rector of Lincoln, Mark Pattison. One story about him will do – a kind of nightmare tutorial which, reworked, will make a good general anecdote for use on Oxbrites who don't know it. Pattison was standing on the hearthrug, with his back to the grate, chatting away, when there was a timid knock on the door, and an undergraduate entered with an essay in his hand. Pattison beckoned the man to come forward, took the sheets of paper and looked over them, puffing slowly at his cigar. Then he crumpled the pages up in his hand, threw them in the man's face and pointed to the door.

Also nineteenth-century was the wretched don who objected to a new gargoyle carved on his college because it was a caricature of himself. The guilty mason changed it – sunk the eyes and hollowed the cheeks. But as the don grew older, he grew to look more and more like the gargoyle.

Trinity, Oxford, isn't famous for much, but a seventeenth-century President called Dr Kettell rather redeems the dull reputation of the college. He used to come into Hall with a pair of scissors hidden in his muff, with which he would cut the hair that he thought to be too long there and then. He had an inventive vocabulary for undergraduate malefactors, too, calling them 'Turds, Tarrarrags (these were the worst sort, rude raskells), Rascal-Jacks, Blindecinques, Scobberlotchers (these did no hurte, were sober, but went idleing about the grove with their hands in their pocketts . . .)'.

Leaving aside Lindsay of Balliol, who, outvoted at council by the fellows at eight votes to one, observed, 'I perceive, gentlemen, that we have reached an impasse', even

But as the don grew older

the shortest canon of dons would be incomplete without Jowett of Balliol (Benjamin Jowett, that is; *not* to be confused with Joseph Jowett, a fellow of Trinity Hall, Cambridge, who composed the quarter-hour chimes for Great St Mary's in 1783. These were cribbed for Big Ben in 1859, and now most unfairly are known as Westminster chimes) and Martin Routh of Magdalen. One comment from each will put you in the picture:

> DON: Master! Something appalling has happened. One of the Fellows has killed himself!
>
> ROUTH: Pray do not tell me who, sir. Allow me to guess.

Jowett (the Jowler) reigned in the latter half of the nineteenth century, and made Balliol the intellectual powerhouse it still (just) remains:

> DON: A priest is more important than a judge. A judge can only say 'You be hanged', but a priest can say 'You be damned'.
>
> JOWETT: Yes, but if a judge says 'You be hanged', you *are* hanged.

Before leaving Oxford which, it must be admitted, does have the better selection of dotty dons, we cannot ignore Spooner. William Spooner was the Warden of New College, 1903–24, so ancient Oxbrites will remember him – just. Everyone knows about the speech impediment which led his name to be enshrined in the *Oxford Dictionary* (under 'spoonerism') in his own lifetime, but few realize that he was *also* an albino. Two indications of his mind will do; *neither* of them spoonerisms, which are very well documented elsewhere:

'In the sermon I have just preached, whenever I said Aristotle, I meant St Paul.'

> SPOONER: Do come to dinner to meet our new fellow, Casson.

FELLOW: But Warden, I *am* Casson.
SPOONER: Never mind, come all the same.

It is worth adding, to Spooner's undying credit, that after the Great War he had a plaque erected in the college chapel commemorating those German members of the college who had fought and died in that war – on the Kaiser's side.

At Cambridge they are little better. Oscar Browning, who was self-centred, gluttonous and brilliant, and who put King's back on its feet at the end of the nineteenth century, had an unfortunate encounter with Lord Tennyson, which is worth trotting out; intellectual Oxbrites, even younger ones, will know about 'OB': It was said that Tennyson, on a visit to Cambridge, had been entertained by the fellows of King's, who came up one by one, mentioning their names. When 'OB' came up and said, "I'm Browning," Tennyson looked at him and said, "You're not."

Older Oxbrites will remember two other Cambridge dons, C. P. Snow and F. R. Leavis. Snow was a scientist who thought himself a novelist; Leavis was a literary critic who thought himself (with some justification) a god. Leavis demolished Snow once, shortly after Snow had coined the famous phrase 'The Two Cultures', at the 1959 Rede Lecture. The Two Cultures, basically Science and Art, were both home to Snow, the scientist/novelist. But Leavis wrote, 'Snow is in fact portentously ignorant ... intellectually as undistinguished as it is possible to be ... The Two Cultures exhibits an utter lack of intellectual distinction and an embarrassing vulgarity of style ... Snow thinks of himself as a novelist. He can't be said to know what a novel is. The nonentity is apparent in every page of his fiction.'

Never forget that Oxbridge is red in tooth and claw.

Never forget either that absent-minded professors *do* exist:

A History don at Trinity, Cambridge: 'Why weren't you at my supervision? Or was it me?'

'I was there, sir, but you weren't.'

(The don looks it up in his terrible handwriting in his diary.) 'Ah, yes; supervision, supervision. Thought it said "shopping", so went shopping instead.'

One don who was not absent-minded deserves a mention. He was Professor Ullmann, Professor of Ecclesiastical History at Trinity. 'There are no Dark Ages,' he would declare. 'I, Ullmann, have made them Light!' As a newcomer to Britain before arriving in Cambridge, he was forced to work for a time as a garage mechanic. Thus it was that Trinity dons developed the habit of taking their cars to the Professor of Ecclesiastical History whenever they broke down.

Dons have been allowed to marry since the end of the last century, as the rash of comfortable villas in North Oxford testifies, but the successful Oxford wife is the one who early accepts that her husband's college is also his mistress. In 1963 Muriel Beadle could still write, 'Once a year we wives were privileged to go to the Master's Lodge, were given an ersatz cup of coffee and a bun, and were allowed to look through a peephole at our husbands in the Hall below, feasting on the fat of the land.'

A final word on dons concerns their dietary habits. The dons themselves, sitting at High Table, generally do themselves well, but the public school tradition, mixed with an English sense of breeding, dictates too that food *may* be from plain to awful, but that wine must always be excellent. All but the poorest colleges have excellent cellars, and the don who is Wine Steward is an authority on his subject. With food finding more favour again after the dreary austerity of most of the twentieth century, and the gradual decay of the keep-fit craze, it may be that soon the tables will once again be graced with such menus as this, eaten at Gonville and Caius for a Bumps Supper at the turn of the century.

Croutes de caviare
Potage à la get-out-at-the-Pike-and-Eel
Blanchailles au Cam
Boudin de Foie Gras aux Truffes
Canard Sauvage à la Ditton Fen
Pouding à la Grassy
Croutes d'Anchois

Wine has never been in abeyance. A modest High Table of only a few years ago might boast:

Meursault Goutte d'Or 1918
Oloroso
Steinberg Cabinet Auslese 1921
Pommery 1921
Romanée Conti 1921
Cockburn 1878
Latour 1920
Cognac Courvoisier 1869

One of the author's informants was privileged as an undergraduate (in 1970) to dine at King's High Table with friendly dons. Once the meal was over (a modest five-courser), he was allowed 'backstage', as it were, to the Wine Room.[1] He was led through a succession of exquisite Georgian rooms to one more beautiful than the rest, reminding him of a small country-house dining room. On the oval Sheraton table in the middle stood silver bowls containing fruit and nuts, and standing in the room were two little walnut-inlay trolleys, each carrying three decanters:

[1] Note the plain name. Oxbridge eschews pretentiousness. Sometimes.

Château Yquem 1948
Mouton Rothschild 1947
Cockburn 1947.

After an agony of indecision, he went for the claret, having been tipped off that stocks of it were beginning to dwindle.

〖7〗

Rules, and how to cope with them

THERE USED TO BE far more rules than there are now, and their passing is mourned, even by the modern Oxbrite, who has brought about their demise, because how can you have fun breaking them if they don't exist? The rules governing the wearing of gowns would fill a book, but though Oxford still clings to that odd robe, Cambridge has virtually given it up for undergraduates. Vestiges do remain, however, because Oxbrites are disinclined to do anything too draconian. A friend of the author who was 'up' in the early seventies remembers having to read the lesson in King's College Chapel, and grabbing the first gown he could find to read it in. Unfortunately he chose an MA's gown, to which he had no right, and was berated for it afterwards, but such occurrences are rare today.

Rules are not what they were. Even the best ones, which 'prohibit important, but perfectly innocent actions, such as smoking in college courts, or walking to Madingley on Sunday without academical dress' (Francis Cornford: *Microcosmographia Academica*), are gone. It is a pity, for, as Francis Cornford, the great Cambridge don, has pointed out 'the merit of such regulations is that, having nothing to do with right or wrong, they help to obscure these troublesome considerations in other cases, and to relieve the mind of all sense of obligation towards society'. You used to have to wear your gown if you went out of college after dark; you used to be excused it if you went for a country walk, but *not* if you passed through any of the town streets in the course of that walk. Nowadays, few of these amiable regulations are enforced any more.

Their disappearance has left a gaping hole in the canon of things Oxbrites like to reminisce about, but most Oxbrites over 30 will still light up when you tackle the question of Climbing In.

In order to pass yourself off as an Oxbrite, you must have at least one Climbing In story. All colleges used to, and some still do, lock their gates at some ungodly early hour, like midnight. Nowadays the inmates have keys, or ring a bell to wake the night porter up. Some modern colleges do not even have walls, or high railings (which ideally are ferociously spiked). Now that most colleges are co-residential, there is no longer any challenge in smuggling a woman or a man back to your rooms. Only a few years ago, however, if you were locked out, or if you wanted to give the *coup de grâce* to a seduction, you had to climb in. Each college had its recognized routes: through the orchard at Jesus, Cambridge; across All Saints' churchyard at Lincoln, Oxford; through the thoughtfully widely spaced railings of the Chapel gate at King's, Cambridge; and over the high but easy grey gate of Memorial Court, Clare. Trinity, Cambridge, had 29 ways of access – two of which were negotiable without dismounting from your bicycle!

Some students had rooms which were 'corridors' for climbers-in and out. One professor left his light on all night to illuminate conveniently an adjacent railing. Dons (who are, it must be said, nearly all sympathetic to everything that is conducive to their peace) were usually kind to climbers-in. A Trinity tutor used to give his new charges maps of the college with the best routes marked on them, and if a don caught you climbing in he would be likely either to unlock the gate for you with his key, or give you a hand in (even if you had a woman with you, and especially if she was wearing a ball gown, for dons are nothing if not chivalrous). A minority of dons were not to

73

be trusted. One Senior Tutor, whose room[1] was a recognized 'corridor', once played a singularly underhand trick. An Oxbrite, having used the familiar window into the room, heard the tutor coming and dived behind the sofa to hide. The tutor entered, and stayed working in the room until the small hours. Only when he finally left did he turn in the doorway and give the 'empty' room an ironical 'good-night'. But poetic justice sometimes pursues such people. A John's don, disturbed by climbers-in near his window, complained to the porters. A porter (my informant) was duly set on night duty to lie in wait. Finally hearing the drunken scrabblings of a climber-in, the porter slunk into the deep shadow of an archway, emerging to trip the passing undergraduate up. Which he did. Only to discover that the sprawling Oxbrite was in fact the complaining don, who, full of claret, had lost his key, and had had to climb in himself.

Normally, climbing in can be performed so safely – even with fourteen pints of Guinness inside you – that all you need worry about is a prowling porter. However, disasters do happen: a Cambridge undergraduate climbing back *in* to Peterhouse with scotch and ciggies to help a late-night *Broadsheet* editorial along, trapped her knees under the barbs of the arrowheads on the gates. Her main worry (truly Oxbridge) was not the *pain*, but the inconvenience of being rusticated, if discovered. She managed to arch her body backwards so that she could slide her legs under the barbs. Her thighs are still scarred, but she didn't drop the scotch. At LMH once a girl was awakened by low groans from near her window. She opened it to see an Oxbrite impaled on the railings. She summoned the porters, who, obedient to the rules, saw to it that college formalities were observed before an ambulance was called, or the Oxbrite (who survived) even unhooked.

[1] 'Room' in this context means 'office', and is not to be confused with 'rooms' (=dwelling). It is important to get this distinction clear.

If anybody tells you a climbing-in story which involves his losing his trousers on the bars, view him with suspicion: he is probably not a true Oxbrite.

Of course Oxbrites break other rules: an amateur but organized drugs ring operated in, of all places, Magdalene, in the early seventies, but it took a police raid to break it; the dons had no idea what was going on. However, since *such* rule-breaking is not quintessentially Oxbridge, it deserves only a passing mention. Dope, pot, shit, hash, grass and, in moneyed circles, coke, are getting to be as bourgeois as port, and are even offered at the end of some dinner parties in lieu of it.

Rules have to have people to make them and to enforce them. Oxbrites themselves are lazy about these, with the exception of the proctors and the Bulldogs already mentioned. To be on the safe side, however, the would-be Oxbrite should be aware of the following:

Rules are called statutes, and sometimes Graces, and often Ordinances. The *old* statutes were built up in a haphazard way, but were licked into shape by Elizabeth I, a much tougher job for her than defeating the Armada. Her statutes lasted until the 1850s after which a series of Commissioners and Acts took place, culminating in the Universities of Oxford and Cambridge Act, 1923, under whose authority the present statutes were made. They can be, and frequently are, amended with the approval of the Queen in Council, and within their limits ordinances can be made ad lib. The Edict, which regulates junior members in residence (*in statu pupillari*[1]), is such a one.

Note that *all* MAs are members of the Senate at Cambridge and the Convocation at Oxford. The Convocation (or the Senate) elects the Chancellor (Oxford and Cambridge), the Professor of Poetry (Oxford) and the High Steward (Cambridge). Nowadays

---

[1] i.e. undergraduate Oxbrites. Easy, isn't it?

Fig. A   Fig. B

YES   NO

allowed to wear nylons

the Chancellor is a figurehead and the true boss is the Vice-Chancellor, elected from the Heads of Houses for two years (or four, depending on where), though the election is a formality since there is a pre-organized line of succession.

The author feels confident that the Oxbridge chain of command is now clear.

Before leaving Rules, a few singling out women alone must be mentioned. The strict days are gone when the enforcement of morality was such that one Oxford girl was sent down for talking to a male cousin in the street, but as late as the early sixties women were not allowed to dine in a men's college Hall, and could be sent down for trying to. Things have now become so lax that women are *officially* allowed to wear lipstick in examinations. However, when nylons were first marketed, and began to supersede the opaque lisle stockings worn before, Oxford elders saw the thin end of a wedge of sexual licence. A committee was formed to deliberate what to do, and finally it passed down this judgement: women would be allowed to wear nylons, *provided that they had a seam up the back.*

⟦8⟧

Customs – totem and taboo

OXBRIDGE HAS A keen sense both of continuity and history, and both are reflected in its traditions. The sense of tradition is strong, and new ones are constantly being introduced, despite the apparently liberal tide. Do not be fooled for a moment into thinking that these traditions are an idle or lugubrious dwelling in the past. Not a bit of it: they are part of the complex code by which Oxbrites recognize one another. Not for nothing did Oxbridge fend off the railway for as long as it possibly could, and then forbid Oxbrites to use it. Keeping the invisible walls that protect Oxbridge from the rest of the world high, and in a good state of repair, is the duty of every Oxbrite.

Almost any excuse will do for a feast. This college custom also finds expression in a host of dining societies (see below, Chapter 11: Social Life I). We will mention some in detail, which Oxbrites of all ages will allude to with pleasure, expecting you to know what they are talking about. Keep at the back of your mind the knowledge that Oxbridge etiquette is Victorian and strict. Always address a Head of House by his or her title, and get it right. Everything will be scrutinized, from the colour of your socks to the way you put your knife and fork down. Be on your guard or be placed forever Beyond the Pale.

But any excuse will do for a feast. The Boar's Head Feast takes place at Queen's on Christmas Night. Basically it was a Christmas Dinner for those northern undergraduates who had too far to travel home over the bad mediaeval roads for the winter vacation, but its origin is not that simple. An undergraduate of the college is supposed to have been attacked by a boar, and to have killed it by shoving a volume of Aristotle down its throat, shouting as he did so (for no apparent reason) 'Graecum est'. Now, every year a boar's head is processed into Hall, heralded by two trumpets, and a carol is sung. The Boar's Head Feast is now a 'Gaudy' (see Chapter 11); but Queen's fields another pretty good feast in February. This is called the 'Needle and Thread' – the name, of course, being a pun on the founder's name: Eglesfield=*aiguille et fil*. Get it? At this dinner, the college bursar presents each guest with a needle and a piece of red thread, exhorting him to thrift. The guest has to pin it onto the lapel of his dinner jacket, and then drink from Eglesfield's loving-cup (made from an auroch's horn – see Chapter 2). What he drinks is a cocktail of secret recipe, known only to the college Steward and his nominated successor. The drink is so powerful that just one draught may actually lay the unsuspecting guest flat on his back.

Examples of Oxbridge obsession with etiquette are the All Souls cherry pie tradition, and sconcing.

The cherry pie story is almost certainly apocryphal, but Oxbrites delight in telling it to each other, amidst fraternal and exclusive chortles almost as disgusting as the story itself. The idea is that each candidate for a Fellowship at All Souls is first invited to dinner with the Fellows there. The pudding is invariably cherry pie, and the candidate succeeds in being, or fails to be, elected, *according to how he disposes of the cherry-stones*. In one version of this story, the bowl in which the pie is served is said to be rimless, further complicating matters. The correct method of disposal is, of course, shrouded in secrecy, but the author can reveal that swallowing the stones is regarded as cheating.

Sconcing has almost died out, but older male Oxbrites will maunder on about it if you let them. Traditionally, talk about women, work or politics (thus neatly covering most areas of conversation) was considered *infra dig* at Hall. If an Oxbrite transgressed, he could be sconced by one of his peers. This meant that he had to drink off a quart of ale (usually from a special silver sconcing cup, or stoup, which looked like a two-handled chamber pot) at a draught. If he succeeded, he could sconce the original sconcer *back*; if he failed, he would have to pay for the beer. A sconce could pass back and forth several times before somebody choked. That somebody would then have to pay for the lot.

Moving away from the table for a moment, the would-be Oxbrite should also be aware of:

St Giles' Fair – held annually in September for two days, when the broad street called St Giles' is closed (Oxford).

The Senate House Leap: a Cambridge initiation ceremony in which the Oxbrite has to jump from the roof of the Senate House to the roof of Gonville and Caius across Senate House Passage. The feat is more bragged about than actually performed, so view people who say they've done it with suspicion.

Climbing the statue of Henry VI in the middle of King's Front Court *without getting caught*. This will entitle you to membership of the Chetwynd Society, and the chance to wear a hideous striped blazer, which any of the university outfitters will run up for you for a modest £300 or thereabouts.

Henry VIII's chairleg: this is verifiable and indeed is often pointed out to tourists. Some desperate Cambridge Oxbrites have even said *they* put it there, to impress rich South American girls from the Mill Road language schools. The fact is this: the statue of Henry VIII on the outside of Trinity Great Court gate bears a chairleg instead of a sceptre. This is owing to a time-honoured undergraduate prank. The authorities once took the chairleg away and restored the sceptre, but the following day the sceptre had gone again – to be replaced by the *same* chairleg.[1]

A word in this section on Rag Weeks. Rags certainly exist at Oxbridge, but they are *out*, and no self-respecting Oxbrite will know much about them. In any case, ordinary universities have them, so they are nothing special. If pressed, mutter something about 'bed races', or even 'slave markets'. These are actually amusing: women would be 'caught' and 'auctioned' for charity in Market Hill, Cambridge. The women would hang about, waiting to be caught, and would be desolate if no one chased them. Then they would be desolate if they felt they weren't fetching a high enough price. You can talk about egg-eating competitions too (inspired by the film *Cool Hand Luke*); and on one occasion there was a home-made beer-drinking competition to support one of the Bishop of Ely's charities – the bishop took the money but was doubtful about the means of getting it. On the whole, though, avoid the subject of Rags in conversation.

Leaving such matters as the Creweian Benefaction and Sporting the Oak to the Glossary, I will move on to two *great* Oxbrite traditions. It may be no coincidence that both have their home at All Souls.

The first is the Betting Book. It is a record of dons' bets with each other, and nothing demonstrates more lucidly the inner workings of the Oxbridge mind. Get into the spirit of this and you will be half way to cracking How to be Oxbridge. Three examples will speak for themselves:

(a) Hardinge bets Reichel 1*s.* that there exists such a tense as τετνφθήσομαί, to which Reichel retorts that that is the grammatical 'paulo-post' as against Hardinge's τετύψομάι (= 'I shall have been on the point of being about to be beaten.')

[1] This story has many variants.

. . . was a black man

(b) Hardinge bets Doyle 1s. that Admiral Benbow was a black man.

(c) Corbett succeeded in proving that he could hang upside-down by the grip of his toes for ten seconds on the Common Room door.[1]

[1] Another linguistic subtlety to beware of: Common Rooms are generally used to smoke, drink and read the papers in. Senior Common Room for fellows, Middle for graduates and Junior for undergraduates (SCR, MCR, JCR); but at Cambridge they are called *Combination* Rooms.

But perhaps the greatest Oxbridge tradition of all is the Ceremony of the Mallard at All Souls. Rumours that its continuance is threatened strike the author as devastating.

The founder of the college, Archbishop Chichele, is supposed to have dreamt that when the foundations of the place were dug, a mallard, 'wele fattened and almost ybosten', would be found in a drain. It was, and the bird has been inexplicably celebrated ever since. Twice a year it is serenaded in a famous song, which must of course never be heard by outsiders' ears.

The *real* ceremony, however, takes place on All Souls' Night. And it takes place only once every hundred years. What happens then is quite something: six Electors nominate a Lord of the Mallard, who will bear the cost of the whole thing. He appoints six officers, who march in front of him carrying white staves, and wearing medals. Carrying the Lord of the Mallard in a kind of sedan chair, and also carrying a dead duck suspended from a pole, everybody then processes three times around the quad, singing the Mallard song at the tops of their voices. They are ritualistically seeking the ghost of the Original Mallard.

Having finished with the quad, they then climb up to the roof and process around that, singing as they go, and carrying torches in front of them. Finally they return to the Common Room and drink a good deal of claret. Then they behead the duck they've been carrying round, and lace a final bumper with its blood. By now it is dawn, and they all go to bed.

The words of the song, as far as I can reveal them, are these:

> Griffin Turkey Bustard Capon
> Let other hungry mortalls gape on
> And on their bones with stomacks fall hard

But let All Souls men have the mallard.
Ho the bloud of King Edward, by ye bloud of King Edward
It was a swapping swapping mallard.

Swapping he was from bill to eye
Swapping he was from wing to thigh
His swapping toole of generation
Out swap'd all the winged Nation.
Ho the bloud . . .

Then let us sing and dance a Galliard
To the remembrance of the mallard
And as the mallard does in Poole
Let's dabble dive and duck in Bowle.
Ho the bloud . . .

The next Mallard ceremony will be on All Souls' Night, 2001.

'When laudable old customs dwindle,' wrote Thomas Hearne, ' 'tis a sign that learning dwindles.' Mind you, he was complaining that they had stopped serving apple fritters for dinner at St Edmund Hall.

[9]

The Rest of Them

NOT ONLY PRINCES of the blood royal like to spend a bit of time at Oxbridge (and Royalty can be rather fickle in its choice: at present, Cambridge is *in*, but Edward VII went to Oxford *and* Cambridge); you can meet a selection of other aristocrats there, too. These still tend to gravitate towards Christ Church at Oxford, but at Cambridge, much to Magdalene's chagrin, and despite the current pretensions of Jesus, Trinity is the place. King's is nowadays considered a little too volatile. Aristocrats tend to stick together, only occasionally going slumming, and then only the more adventurous ones. Getting involved with aristocrats can create its own difficulties. One Girton undergraduate (who had rooms in college but was resourceful enough never to have to use them again after her first term) accepted overtures from an aristo. For a while everything went swimmingly, but inevitably one day Mamma turned up and subjected 'Andrea' to a grilling which would have been the envy of the Special Branch. The thing which annoyed 'Andrea' most was that the mother assumed *ipso facto* that she had marital designs on her little boy. Since the aristo was beginning to tire her anyway, she ditched him soon afterwards. No one, she later learned, was more aggrieved about this than Mamma, who had after all approved.

If you're not an aristocrat, you may at least be from a public school. Girls' public schools carry little cachet at Oxbridge, which has not yet reconciled itself to no longer being a male bastion (indeed it is still kicking, if you will pardon the expression, against the pricks). Boys' public schools still ride high. There are specific connections between Westminster and Christ Church; Winchester and New College; Eton and King's; and Merchant Taylors' and St John's, Oxford. These do not necessarily follow as of right to quite the same extent as they did, but it still certainly helps to have been to one of the dozen or so first and second rank public schools. The advantages this confers are not necessarily the obvious ones, such as Good Connections. Rather, people coming up to Oxbridge from such backgrounds will find less to adjust to because they are used to:

(a) being away from home (boarding school)
(b) ancient traditions
(c) occasionally having to wear odd clothes for ceremonies
(d) bad food
(e) freezing beds.

Public school can also confer the advantage of instant companionship, since at most good public schools you are educated up to the hilt, and thus more of you are likely to get into Oxbridge. You do have a lot of advantages, fair or not, and the average Oxbridge fresher from Bedales or Repton or Marlborough is more likely to be going up in the company of some of his schoolfellows than someone from Eltham Green Comprehensive.

Many people have described their first night at Oxbridge as the loneliest in their lives. Dudley Moore, who went up to Oxford from a very ordinary school indeed, says it took him a year to get into the swim of things. His experience is pretty typical, because if you come up from a grammar school, or worse, you will be in for some severe shocks to the system, because you will probably be used to:

(a) home cooking
(b) the company of women (at least this was true

pre-1974, when women really started to figure at Oxbridge; and even today . . .)

(c) warmth.

It is quite possible that you will not have worn a dinner jacket before; you may never have eaten in a Chinese restaurant; you may never have been away from the comfort of your mother's side! Many of the dining clubs will be closed to you, and even the most democratic societies will frown on you unless you work hard to make your mark. Thus it is that many people from ordinary schools are socially *grey*, and join the Tiddlywinks Society or the Dungeons and Dragons Club. Unless, that is, they are stunningly beautiful, or have wit and courage, or simply *Do Not Care*.

Oxbrites from ordinary schools should *not* be daunted. Oxbrites who write about Oxbridge in later life nearly always give a false impression; their view is either too rose-tinted or too jaundiced, or just put across as a jumble of Oxbridge clichés. Beware of plays and novels about Oxbridge for these reasons. Oxbridge had a highly stratified society before 1939, but after 1945 that was beginning to crumble fast. However, as it did, the imperative to build bulwarks against the World Outside dictated that the old presentation should live on – and it did; it lived on in myth, and was even recreated as myth – wrapped in a kind of sentimental cellophane.

In the World Outside, using the Oxbridge connection to climb the ladder is successful in direct ratio to the élan with which you play your cards. This is a trick inculcated at Oxbridge, where Oxbrites are encouraged:

(a) to be very competitive
(b) to think the world is their oyster.

Unfortunately these two ideas do not sit well together, which is why most Oxbrites meeting each other later on get the 'how do you dos' out of the way very quickly, and, pricing their interlocutor's house/car/wife/husband/soft furnishings with their eyes, move on to the Most Important Question: 'How are you getting on?'

People who didn't go to either place sometimes thank God that they didn't, because to an innocent outsider Oxbrites *sound* so fiercely competitive: in fact of course it's just a collection of bums jostling each other for room on the bench, exactly like anywhere else. Realizing this is another question. Most people don't, at least for a while, and *in extremis* some Oxbrites go under, and shoot themselves.

Most colleges now make it a policy for freshers to spend their first year in residence, because living alone in digs on the edge of town can be a terrifying experience, especially if you've never been away from home before. The mere fact that suddenly, at 18 or 19, with no warning, you are left to make your own decisions and take responsibility for your own actions, is bad enough. No wonder people take to cementing chamber pots to chapel spires.

It is difficult to break down the social frontiers. Trinity, Cambridge, organizes things quite successfully by arranging for freshmen from different backgrounds to share rooms. Clare nowadays goes further and allows people of different sexes to share rooms. The fact is that none of this rocks the Oxbridge boat. One American visitor to Oxford pointed out that anything that's generally true of England is exaggerated at Oxbridge: this would be fine if there *were* anything that was *generally* true. The problem is that there are so few general truths to dig up and isolate. And that is half the fun, too.

It is, however, sometimes a bit difficult for the Foreigner; and it is this group which we must turn our attention to next.

Oxford took its first black American undergraduate in 1907; it took its second in 1963. That is nothing. Women undergraduates weren't eligible for Rhodes Scholarships until 1977. In the last few years enormous changes have come out of what was effectively the melting pot of the sixties, and now there are plenty of foreign students,[1] of all shapes, sizes and races at Oxbridge. For them, the place is of value less for its social than its academic life, although an Indian acquaintance of the author remembers going up to Cambridge just after an expedition to K2, and enjoying the expression on the faces of the Climbing Club's committee when he joined and told them that, yes, he had been higher than 2,000 feet. American students are often used to universities with their own 'real' radio and tv stations, and theatres which would be the envy of many large towns. They retreat in disgust from the mean comparable facilities Oxbridge offers, and hide in their books.

It is not, however, only material things which worry them. Students from erstwhile colonies have no trouble at all, because they know how quirky the English can be, and can view them with amused detachment while getting as much as possible out of the opportunities offered; but erstwhile English *colonists*, such as Americans and Australians, sometimes find it hard to come to terms with the roots they have come from, preserved in amber as they are at Oxbridge. A highly distinguished Dartmouth History major whom I shall call 'Peter' decided to read PPE at University College, Oxford, from 1970–4, rather than go to the Harvard Business School. He was appalled at the snobbery of the English class system he saw in operation – 'working-class kids were just ostracized' – and found his friends amongst fellow Americans, Scotsmen (who took a healthy 'sod the English' line), the son of the Prime Minister of Ghana and 'Pinkie' Bhutto (the daughter of the late Pakistani statesman). He also made

[1] There would be more if they were not obliged nowadays to pay their own way.

89

friends with Lloyd George's grandson, and a man whose father had cornered the world market in tapioca. However, he only joined the Union Society for the movies – he was too intimidated by it to speak at debates. Subsequently he has been invited back there as a guest speaker.

'Peter' came to Oxford on a Keasbey Scholarship. This is one of several such scholarships available to American would-be Oxbrites: there's also the Reynolds, the Marshall and, probably the best known, the Rhodes.

Cecil Rhodes was at Oriel and he made such a lot of money from all his diamond mines that when he died in 1902 he was able to leave £4,000,000 for the foundation of 150–200 perpetual scholarships at Oxford. You had to be red hot to get one: 'I direct that in the election of a student to a scholarship regard shall be had to ... his qualities of manhood truth courage devotion to duty sympathy for the protection of the weak kindliness unselfishness and fellowship.' (Among other things.) Foreigners from all the Commonwealth countries, from the USA and from West Germany are eligible. Some people jib at the thought of taking money from such a source as Cecil, but most accept gratefully. Rhodes House, which was built in 1928, has a no-smoking notice on its entrance-hall floor. True to Oxbridge tradition, the notice reads:

ΜΗΔΕΙΣ ΚΑΠΝΟΦΟΡΟΣ ΕΙΣΙΤΩ.

We have seen that Cambridge Oxbrites tend to prefer, where possible, women undergraduates to women from outside the university, and that at Oxford the reverse is true. Before a much fuller and more balanced account (see below, Chapter 12: Social Life II), we must consider the Other Women Available.[1]

[1] Women undergraduates have boyfriends at home/in London, or go for male undergraduates, graduates and younger dons only. In any case, they are spoilt for choice.

Owing to the traditional lack of women within the two universities, female company has often been sought from outside. From what I can gather, the Oxford woman undergraduate presents such a daunting front that she drives her male counterparts from her. Simultaneously she regrets this, and feels left out. It is a vicious circle which I hope somebody will break soon. It does not appear to happen at Cambridge. Meanwhile, male Oxford undergraduates may find solace in the following alternative areas:

First of all, there are the secretarial colleges. Chief of these are St Aldate's and the Marlborough, but perhaps the best known is the Oxford and County Secretarial College at 34, St Giles', and conveniently next door to the Army Careers Information Centre. This has been described elsewhere as a refuge of Sloanes in search of a husband, and the truth of this is borne out by my informants who tell me that 'Ox and Cow' women do rather like to 'grab a Christ Church man if they can'. Women from secretarial schools are generally to be met in the Chequers pub, a town and gown establishment with a loud juke-box off the High. Don't be bashful about approaching them – they gather here specifically to be picked up.

The second main group of non-university women who can influence the Oxford Oxbrite is that from the crammer and the finishing school. Beech Lawn, Green's and Wolsey Hall are examples of these, and the finished product has been mentioned with approval by my informants. Beech Lawn is especially attractive because of its high proportion of rebellious upper-class public school girls.

The third and fourth groups affect all male Oxbrites: they are nurses and language school women. Nurses come in all shapes and sizes from Addenbrooke's in Cambridge and the Radcliffe Infirmary at Oxford. St Giles' pubs are the place to meet them at Oxford, but at Cambridge you will have to venture rather far from the centre of town. Language school women are a nebulous bunch, usually very wealthy but proportionately dim, more often than not coming from the further-flung Spanish-speaking nations – and heavily in search of a husband.

Adventurous Oxford Oxbrites may even care to approach townie women – though adventurous Cambridge Oxbrites need not attempt this. At Oxford, the best place to do it was traditionally White's Bar near Carfax. 'It was good for picking up town scrubbers, and it had plastic fountains,' one Oxbrite remembers. A drawback to White's Bar was that it was also the haunt of 'toughies from the motor trade', which made it a good place for fighting too. 'It was a dire gin palace,' recalls my informant, affectionately.

Oxford Town Hall will occasionally host dances, sometimes still called 'hops', which are downmarket, all-comers affairs, and which are Mecca to aspiring town women, desperate male Oxbrites, and finishing school girls who have had no luck elsewhere. It should be remembered that, by and large, the Oxbrite who opts for a non-Oxbrite partner *during his time at Oxbridge* is courting disaster; by the same token Oxbrites who marry other Oxbrites in the World Outside generally take their lives in their hands. For more on this, see below, Chapter 12: Social Life II.

Townies in general have been dealt with. By and large they have their own part of town, their own pubs and restaurants, which the Oxbrite should respect (but generally doesn't). Do not court townies' friendship because that will be taken at best as condescension and at worst as homosexual overture. If a townie offers you the hand of friendship, treat it with the suspicion it deserves: he may be setting you up. On this traditional understanding,

Town and Gown cohabit (see above, Chapter 3: Town versus Gown).

Within your college, you will encounter a category of person which owes nothing to background. They are not usually ex-public school, but can be as dreadful in a different way. These are the 'grey men/women' (Cambridge) or 'gnomes' (Oxford). Enoch Powell was one once. Such people are grimly and totally dedicated to work, and many avoid social life completely – sometimes to the extent of sleeping by day and working by night (though some are forced to be diurnal because of lectures). Often they lock their doors, and pretend to be out when you call. One such grey man was 'Derek': he had excellent rooms, freshly painted and newly furnished. Perfect for parties and seductions. He put them to no use whatsoever. He introduced not a single book into them, let alone a poster or a picture. An Oxbrite remembers going to see him one day to ask when the next train to London was, and finding him all alone in his totally bare rooms, sitting at a table eating cold baked beans from a saucer with a teaspoon. 'Derek's' hobby was memorizing out-of-date train timetables. He could tell you effortlessly how to get from Edinburgh to Devizes in August 1931. He is now a senior administrator with British Rail.

Grey men are nothing to fear. They will leave you alone if you leave them alone. Occasionally they may feel the need to come out of their shells and then they may buttonhole you and bore you for hours over lukewarm Nescafé and rich tea biscuits about such things as the Determination of Natural Mortality and its Causes in an Exploited Population of Cockles. But this is probably the worst that they can do.

You will also have to deal with Hearties, Hacks and Cogs. Hearties are usually associated with sport (though you can get theatre hearties too) and are almost always male. You can recognize them by their habit of standing around in large groups drinking far too much beer, upon which some of them profess to be Authorities. Hearties are therefore bores, and frequently boors too, and are better avoided. Luckily they tend to remain in their own circles, but beware of them if you encounter them in drunken gangs at night, or (worse) after Bumps if their boat has won, when they can be murderous. Oxbrites keen on furthering their careers should, however, be cautious of denouncing hearties in unfamiliar company in the World Outside. Many a company director has been a hearty in his youth – and proud of it. Theatre hearties are less dangerous than sporty hearties, but can transmit a sensation of boredom strong enough to bend forks with. Sporting hearties can be conveniently divided up into beefheads, or boaties, who row; and ruggerbuggers, who play Rugby *Union*, the two divisions reflecting the two principal university sports. Female Oxbrites also row these days, and well; but they have not yet developed Heartiness.

The technical term 'hack' will not be familiar to older Oxbrites in *this* sense. It is applied to those who are bent on gathering material, experience and contacts for their future career while still at Oxbridge. This used to be regarded as *in*, but nowadays it is thought to be *out*. The three areas particularly populated by hacks are: journalism (*Isis*, *Cherwell*, *Tributary* at Oxford, *Stop Press*, *The Heckler*, *Broadsheet* at Cambridge); politics (Oxford and Cambridge Union Societies); and the theatre (OUDS and ETC at Oxford, ADC and Footlights at Cambridge).[1]

A 'cog' is what every Oxbrite would hope to be. Cogs are *cognoscenti* – thoroughly integrated, *in* people, who know exactly what clubs to belong to, what pubs to drink

[1] Do not worry about all these names. They will be dealt with below, in Chapter 11: Social Life I.

Great Cambridge Mind

at, and what clothes to wear. Their success with the opposite sex is effortless, and their passage through Oxbridge flawless. Beware of self-styled cogs; the genuine article unfortunately only exists in theory.

Finally we come to GCMs, GOMs and GLFs. Great Cambridge Minds and Great Oxford Minds are rare creatures, often more spoken of than actually seen. Early examples of the genuine article are Bertrand Russell, G. E. Moore and Wittgenstein (GCMs); F. A. Lindemann, W. H. Auden and Oscar Wilde (GOMs). The *crucial* thing is that you can *only* refer to GCMs and GOMs who were contemporaries of yours; this you can do with a mixture of awe (to engender respect for them) and familiarity (to engender respect for yourself). Oxbrites will still frequently play this trick, years and years after they have come down. The desired effect is the implantation of the respectful thought, 'God, he was up at Oxbridge with ——'. The non-Oxbrite will immediately assume that you were on intimate terms with the GCM or GOM, and be impressed. The Oxbrite can then bask in reflected splendour, or reap the benefits of his con: the person he has impressed is not to know that he probably never in fact even *saw* the GCM or GOM. At best he might have passed him in the street. One anecdote illustrates this: an Oxbrite up at Cambridge with Prince Charles (not quite a GCM, but his example will serve) once passed him in Senate House Passage. He noted what the Prince was wearing, how big he was and so on. Thus for years after he was able to dine out on comments like, 'Charlie? Oh, yes, always wore loud check sports jackets and grey slacks. Much bigger than he looks on television.' He had people eating out of his hand. Salman Rushdie taught an Oxbrite acquaintance of the author to punt. This is true, and the inference is that the Oxbrite must be an intimate of the GCM in question. But this is not true, as they have not met for over fifteen years.

Luminaries are a miniature form of the GCM/GOM. Jonathan Miller and Sir Peter Hall are good examples. The same rules apply in alluding to them.

GLFs, or Godlike Figures, are far less substantial creatures. GLFs are usually socialites or theatrical. More often than not they are in their final year when you are in your first year, and if they deign to speak to you at all, it will be to humiliate you. Bide your time. In all probability, in the World Outside these same GLFs will come crawling to you for work.

Again, the GLFs you are allowed to reminisce about are *ones who were contemporaries of yours*. Note that not all of them are bad; they just like to concentrate on being GLFs all the time. Before leaving them for the moment, a note of caution about them must be sounded: although many GLFs fall flat on their faces in the World Outside, and thus cease to be Useful, just as many have such dynamic egos that they *succeed* in the World Outside (especially in journalism and television), and continue to be GLFs. These people are often insufferable, since they never notice that Oxbridge and the World Outside are two different places, and continue through life in a kind of delayed adolescent haze. Nevertheless, contemporary GLFs should never be lost sight of. Years later you can approach them with a cheery, 'Hi, X, remember me? I'm Y. We were in Footlights together.' If you are lucky, the frosty stare will be replaced by a three-millimetre smile; but your success thereafter will be in proportion to how useful the GLF thinks you will be to him *now*.

⟦10⟧

Dress Sense – costume drama

BEFORE GOING ON to the finer points, the first matter to settle is that of gowns, and the function of gowns these days. It is ironic that Cambridge has all but abandoned them, since it undoubtedly has classier ones. There are, of course, dozens of different types of gown, according to the academic rank of the wearer, and the kind of degree he holds. Undergraduates have gowns too, and these may vary according to whether he is a Scholar, or a Commoner/Pensioner. Exhibitioners[1] do not have special gowns, and there is no distinction between undergraduate gowns on this level at Cambridge. At Oxford, male Exhibitioners at some colleges may wear Scholars' gowns; female Exhibitioners, however, wear Commoners' gowns.

At Oxford, undergraduates' gowns do not differ from college to college. At Cambridge, they all do. All undergraduate gowns are black, except for Trinity, Cambridge and Caius, which are blue. Cambridge Pensioners' gowns look not unlike Oxford Scholars' gowns, except that their sleeves are grander and more billowy. They are worn knee-length. Oxford Commoners' gowns are ghastly little rags which are hardly worth wearing at all. They barely cover the wearer's bottom, have no sleeves, and are decorated with ridiculous streamers which have square pleating on their upper halves and hang the full length of the gown. Tradition has it that these streamers, or 'tapes', were put there for the

---

[1] An Exhibitioner is one who has won an 'exhibition' to his college – see p. 41 and Glossary.

convenience of proctors or creditors (i.e. townie tradesmen) to grab errant undergraduates by.

The best gowns of all are the Chancellors'. They are made of black brocaded silk (most other gowns are made of Russell cord or rayon nowadays), and are covered with gold lace trimmings. The cap has a gold tassel, and is made of black velvet.

Not *all* gowns are black: red, crimson and cerise, grey and blue, and mixtures thereof are not uncommon. An Oxford Doctor of Music wears a fetching little number made up of cream silk with apple-blossom embroidery, with facings and sleeves of cherry crimson silk, the whole topped off with a black bonnet. It is not my intention to go into all the arcane byways of gowns here: there simply isn't space. Nor am I going to deal with the whole question of *hoods*, and their significance, except to say that they are never worn *up*. Most Oxbrites themselves will be vague on the full intricacy of academic wear. Remember how to describe your own undergraduate gown, and unless you are a career academic, that will be more than adequate. Most Oxbrites do not care about gowns after they have come down (although one of my acquaintance used to make her husband dress up in hers for various intimate purposes in later life), and most never wear the gown of their degree, since they are not entitled to wear it until after they have graduated, by which time they have all but left the university, and have set their minds to other things, such as getting a job.

Before leaving the question of gowns, a word must be given on the important subject of subfusc. The ordinary Oxbrite only ever wears this once (to take his degree) at Cambridge (and not even then if he takes his degree by proxy), but Oxonians wear it to matriculate, and to sit exams as well. Subfusc is:

FOR MEN:

a dark suit (a dinner jacket will do), dark socks, dark

99

'subfusc'

footwear, white shirt, white collar and white bow-tie (at Cambridge an upright collar is favoured, and white bands are worn as well as the tie).

FOR WOMEN:
a white blouse, black tie, dark skirt or trousers, black stockings, dark footwear and (optional) a dark coat.
– all this in addition to the cap (Oxford only) and gown.

Do *not* attempt, as one Oxbrite of my acquaintance did, to proceed to your degree wearing a white tie and collar cut out of cardboard (though in fact he got away with it); nor, as he did, say 'Ta, mate' to the Vice-Chancellor once he has conferred your degree upon you. That Simply Does Not Do. In any case the Vice-Chancellor put him down immediately by replying, 'You're welcome'.

Degree-giving should also be mentioned here, since you will have to know about it, and it has as much to do with dressing up and gowns as anything. Ordinary Oxbrites take their degrees in June or early July, in the Sheldonian Theatre at Oxford and the Senate House at Cambridge. Everything is in Latin, which is the official language of Oxbridge. Don't worry, nowadays many Oxbrites themselves can't speak a word of it. It is nerve-racking, but you get through it – it's certainly no worse than getting married. You're 'introduced' to the Vice-Chancellor by a don called a praelector. He's a member of your college (he's also known as the Father of the College), and he will have drilled you beforehand. You have nothing to say, if you're just up for the first time. The praelector introduces you in groups of four, which is awkward, since each of you has to cling to one finger of his hand (but *not* the thumb), as he does so. Then, one by one, up you go, kneel, place your hands between the Vice-Chancellor's, have the formula mumbled over you, and out you go into the sunshine to be congratulated by grinning tutors, supervisors etc., and presented with your final term's *battels* (or bill).

BATTELS

Of course all this is a gross oversimplification: gownsmanship and the art of taking degrees form keystones in the invisible wall that separates Oxbridge from the Rest. But what has been described will be more than adequate to cover you in the unlikely event of the talk turning to such things in Oxbrite circles in the World Outside. If someone says, 'But didn't he dot you on the head with a bible, too?', furrow your brow and drink some more sherry. Or counter with the bit about Henry the son of Simeon (see above, Chapter 3). A good deal of bowing, curtsying and kneeling goes on at degree taking, and at Oxford especially a number of proctors and Bedels (not to be confused with Bedells, of course), get in on the act too. It's all too much for anyone to remember in detail, so don't worry. Oxford Oxbrites who want to go into this question should read: *The Oxford Degree Ceremony* by J. Wells (Clarendon Press, 1906), and *Oxford University Ceremonies* by L. H. Dudley Buxton and Strickland Gibson (Clarendon Press, 1935). Both these worthy tomes are now, however, sadly out of print.

The ordinary summer degree day is called General Admissions at Cambridge; but the height of Oxbridge academic ceremony must be the Encaenia (soft 'c'), or Commemoration, held on the Wednesday following the end of Trinity term at Oxford. This junket confers honorary degrees on eminent Oxbrites and non-Oxbrites who have made it big in the World Outside.

The Encaenia features the Chief Constable, the University Marshal, the University Verger, some Bedels, the Chancellor, the High Steward, the Vice-Chancellor and proctors, the Assessor, the Public Orator, the Professor of Poetry – one of these last two makes the Creweian Oration – and the Registrar. It is preceded by strawberries and champagne, thanks to the Creweian Benefaction, and afterwards the Vice-Chancellor gives a garden party, at which everyone wears academic dress, *but* instead of white ties, ordinary ties are worn.

Which brings us to the whole question of ties. It is one which women are mercifully released from. Ties in general are *in*, but rapidly moving *out* again (they were very much *in* in the mid to late seventies), but it is important to realize that it is not the wearing of a tie *per se* that matters; it is *what* tie you wear and *when* you wear it. Ties as a mark of belonging somewhere are not exclusively Oxbridge: old school ties, and club and regimental ties, and even company ties, can be seen around conforming necks everywhere. 'By his tie shall ye know him' has been an English byword for at least a century.

At Oxbridge, the university outfitters will provide you with the following array:

college ties (crested)
college ties (striped)
college ties (summer)
club ties
university ties (very rarely seen)

The number and variation are great. One important rule applies to all of them: never wear them.

It is difficult to avoid owning them. Proud parents will buy them for you unbidden. Accept them gracefully and then put them away.

The reason for this is simple: the true Oxbrite does not advertise himself, because he does not feel he needs to. Self-advertisement is the refuge of the socially and intellectually insecure. So never wear any tie of affiliation.

However, like all rules, this is not quite so simple. Although no such ties should be worn whilst the Oxbrite is 'up' at Oxbridge,[1] he may in the World Outside, but preferably only later in life, wear *club* ties. A Footlights tie (especially hideous – two shades of maroon, and light blue) can work wonders in the right circles, for example. *But*: never wear any such tie when going for an interview (it looks like begging at best, snobbery at worst), and never, *never* wear your college tie, *ever*. This is the mark of the greyest of grey men: wear one, and you will either be accounted a bore by anonymous Oxbrites who notice it and avoid you, or you will attract boring Oxbrites who take you for one of them. I can only find one example of a college tie being worn with style and this was when the actor Jack Hulbert wore his Gonville and Caius tie in *The Spider's Web*, his first film, in which he appeared as an extra. ·

The only ties that may be worn with impunity are those which 'advertise' worthy causes, like the World Wildlife Fund, or the Royal Society for the Protection of Birds – but even they should not be 'overworked'.

Ties can get you into trouble in other ways. 'Oscar' was a colonial medical student at Caius in the fifties. He wore his old school tie one day, and was asked about it by a

[1] Except, of course, on special occasions, such as club dinners, where full club regalia may be worn: special tie (usually bow), blazer and waistcoat, for example. See more, below.

fellow student (an Etonian) over a corpse they were dissecting together. The tie in question bore a white rose on a dark blue background. The conversation went like this:

E : Couldn't help noticing your tie, old chap.
O: Oh?
E : Yes. Yorkshire C.C.?
O: Er – no. St Edmund's.
E : St *Ed*mund's. Didn't realize. You must have known Harry Wallenstein-Plumrose.
O: No. St Edmund's, Kenya.
   (*Pause*)
E : Oh.
   (*Silence*)

No discussion of ties would be complete without mention of one of the most appalling of all, now happily merely a collector's item. Older Cambridge Oxbrites will remember 'The King Street Run'. Completing this meant downing a pint of bitter in every one of a large number of pubs in King Street, a dingy causeway behind the town centre. You had to complete the course 'against the clock', and to help you, your friends would run ahead to set your pint up for you, and some of the more unscrupulous would not be above having a double vodka slipped into it for good measure. If you managed to drink your fourteen pints or so within the time limit, you earned the right to wear a blue tie, bearing a silver tankard with the letters KSR under it in gold. Near the bottom of the tie, silver Ps were stitched – one for every time you had puked. Fortunately, King Street was practically demolished in the seventies, and the true Run is no longer possible – though one pub which survives in the street, formerly the Horse and Groom, has recently and vulgarly been renamed the King Street Run by the brewers, Whitbread. To the author's disgust, this pub serves good beer, and is popular.

The King Street Run

Bow versions of club ties are available, and these *are* acceptable wear, *but only while you are 'up'*, and only at club functions and dinners. Then they may be worn either with dj and a special waistcoat (e.g. the Patriarchs, at Oxford), or with the matching blazer (e.g. the Chetwynd; the Footlights, Cambridge). Special club waistcoats are usually available for a fairly modest price from those university outfitters who specialize in college wear, such as Hall's (the High) and Castell's (the Broad) in Oxford, and Ryder and Amies, Roper's or, for the really rich, Ede and Ravenscroft, in Cambridge. Blazers can be made to order too, although today fewer and fewer are seen since, as I have noted, a really special variegated number could set you back £300 these days.

After ties come scarves. Scarves are the mark of the grey man or gnome, and worse besides: college scarves are beloved of students of ordinary universities, and even (horrors!) of polytechnics. Avoid them at all costs; no true Oxbrite would be seen dead in one, at least any Oxbrite of later than 1963 vintage. Before that time it was eccentric, but perfectly acceptable, to wear one with your duffle coat. 'Aloysius', mentioned above, decided to buy one in conscious defiance of this unwritten rule of good taste; but he found that in practice he never wore the thing at all.

Finally a note of dire warning. Most university outfitters display for sale college crest emblems mounted on wood, crested cufflinks and even crested tie-clips. To buy, wear or display any of these immediately forfeits the perpetrator's right to be Oxbridge for ever. The zealous would-be Oxbrite should strenuously beware of such traps. The crested writingpaper, cigarettes and sherry that the college butteries sell are, however, perfectly fine, *provided that they are only used* in situ.

Having settled the matter of gowns, ties and scarves, it is now necessary to move into the more nebulous area of personal appearance.

When John Ruskin went up to Oxford in 1836 he had to swear before the Vice-Chancellor 'not to cut or comb my hair fantastically'. This oath harked back 200 years to when William Laud, Archbishop of Canterbury and Chancellor of the University (Chancellors had more power in those days), sorted out all the rules and statutes of the university. Laud must have had a very strong mind indeed not to crack under the strain of it all, and he produced the Laudian Code, which was effective until 1864 and left no stone unturned:

> It is enacted that all the heads, fellows and scholars of colleges, as well as all persons in holy orders, shall dress as becomes clerks. Also that all others (except the sons of barons having the right of voting in the Upper House of Parliament, and also of barons of the Scotch [sic] and Irish peerages) shall wear dresses of a black or dark colour, and shall not imitate anything betokening pride or luxury, but hold themselves aloof from them. Moreover they shall be obliged to abstain from that absurd and assuming practice of walking publicly in boots. There must be, also, a mean observed in the dressing of the hair; and they are not to encourage the growth of curls, or immoderately long hair.

The statutes have relaxed since those days; a male Oxbrite quite recently stencilled a 'Grateful Dead' logo to the back of his gown and there was nothing in the statutes to touch him. But despite the relaxation of rules on dress, hair and so on, it is interesting to note that Oxbrites only follow fashion up to a point. You will find no absolute pop star lookalikes or outright punks, no hippy or teddy-boy throwbacks among Oxbrites; or if there is *one*, he is the exception that proves the rule. Only in the sixties was any real concession made to prevailing fashion; but then, in the sixties fashion prevailed everywhere far more than it has ever done since.

For the most part, Oxbridge women wear their hair longer than it is currently fashionable to do, but in that shoulder-length style which men *always* find attractive; and Oxbridge men wear their hair medium length by choice. Beards and moustaches, which swept the country in the sixties and seventies, are now *out*, except on Oxbrites in the 28–38 age range, who have probably retained them. Oxbridge women show an extraordinary loyalty to:

(a) the 'midi'
(b) Laura Ashley
(c) Indian cotton.

This is largely due to the fact that Oxbridge women develop large thighs owing to cycling too much, and favour long things to cover the ravages of Nature. Sloanes are the same. *Their* thighs come from riding too much in early youth.

Oxbridge men for the past 15–20 years have worn variations on the limited, but cheap and practical, 'jeans and pullover' look. Most, unless they are forced into suits in the World Outside, retain this habit of dress to the grave. Local variations should be noted, and a brief decade-by-decade guide is given below. The guide is broad, and applicable only to 'average' dress. Variations are given later:

Fifties

HE:
cavalry twill trousers
tweed jackets (*risqué*)
lumberjack shirts
not suede shoes
obscure club ties
SHE:
pencil-line giving way on occasion to bell-tent skirt
one-colour blouse with some discreet frills
very chunky pullovers
very tight black slacks
short coats with huge buttons

(At this period it was still just acceptable to wear college ties and scarves. Male habits included pipe-smoking and wearing duffle coats. Black rollneck pullovers, black

Fifties

HE   SHE

trousers and jeans were just entering the consciousness of the truly avant-garde.)

Sixties

HE:
jeans/bell-bottoms/flares
box-cut jackets

rollnecks
ex-RAF leather jackets
corduroy shirts
ex-army greatcoats
desert boots
snappy suits
Levi cord suits
SHE:
jeans, slacks
mini (predominantly), midi and maxi skirts and dresses
big-pattern shirts
long dark scarves
chunky jewellery made of plastic
black lace tights
leather boots

(Girls' hair was worn long, or up in sexy wispy academic buns, or in cool Quant and Sassoon cuts; eye make-up was heavy. Men began to grow a variety of facial hair. Liverpudlians were in demand, sex came out of the closet – at Oxbridge, as everywhere.)

Seventies

HE:
a return to the jacket and slacks look, finally resolving itself into pullovers and jeans
SHE:
a return to more conventional clothes, finally resolving itself into pullovers and jeans

(After the false dawn of the sixties, Oxbrites (a) swung to the right, and (b) became less interested in politics anyway. Work crept *in*, as a respect for the World Outside and a desire to come to terms with it gradually replaced the old sixties contempt for it.)

Eighties

HE:

open-necked shirt
pullover (Marks and Spencer; non-patterned, usually grey or other dark colour, crew neck, longsleeved)
clean but battered jeans
white socks (or dark blue which show dirt less)
trainers – Nike or Adidas

SHE:

Very similar

A footnote should be added to the guide above. In the sixties, many Oxbrites who dressed relatively conventionally most of the time, have confessed to the author that they also had a 'secret wardrobe', comprising dirty pullovers and jeans, which they used to wear to Anarchist Society meetings, and similar functions. A wave of dirt, remembered with appropriate disgust by middle-aged dons, was apparent in the early seventies. It featured essentially tattered jeans and sweaty sweatshirts, and hair was worn matted. This phase was shortlived and not general.

So much for what the average Oxbrite wears. Note that Levis, Wranglers[1] and so on dominate leg wear, and Marks and Spencer dominate pullover and underwear. If that all sounds a little dull, do not despair. There is plenty of scope for eccentricity, and a little research will tog you up in a Tennysonian black hat and an undertaker's cloak. Worn with a luminous scarf, this would be considered more than chic for attending a Tolkien Society meeting. A variety of brocade waistcoats and natty canes can be bought at university outfitters, and if your budget won't

---

[1] Not, of course, to be confused with Wranglers, Senior and Junior Optimes, which are classes of pass in the Cambridge Mathematics Tripos.

run to them, or you prefer a different image, you can try the second-hand stalls at the market (Cambridge), or various downmarket and army-surplus stores in Oxford. One Cambridge Oxbrite of my acquaintance invariably wore a black frock-coat, black pin-striped trousers, black shoes and socks, a black brocade waistcoat, a black silk shirt and cravat, the ensemble completed with a black opera cloak and a black shaggy velvet borsalino.

Grey Oxbrites dress with less élan, but for purposes of identification their clothing must be described. Standard wear for males is:

sports jacket (preferably from Burton or John Collier)
nylon shirt (vest visible beneath)
terylene college or old school tie
brown terylene trousers
grey socks (sagging)
tan or black moccasin-style shoes
college scarf (optional).

Females of this type are less easily identifiable externally, though their manner will be found to be unmistakable. A variant on the grey theme is the grey scientist, who will be found in:

woolly hat
parka
sagging pullover
open-necked nylon shirt
jeans (concertina'd at the knee)
'Wallabee' or 'Polyveldt' shoes.

The moment of real Oxbridge glory is the end of the Trinity/Easter term, when a large number of cocktail parties take place idyllically on lawns; when you punt up and down on the river with the partner of your choice; and when you go to Balls. All this provides a marvellous excuse for donning everything from turbans with peacock feathers to coffee cream silk double-breasted suits with matching hat and shoes. Never again does an Oxbrite preen to quite such an extent, or derive more pleasure from it.

Men have it easier than women because most of the Balls simply demand Black Tie (only a very few are exceptions and expect White Tie); women on the other hand have far more fun. Your ball gown is probably going to give you greater pleasure and longer service than your wedding dress ever will (even converted), if you are a true Oxbrite. Choose it with almost as much care as you choose your partner. The shops are there to cater for you; indeed they are past masters, which is why some of the best clothes shops in England for both sexes are to be found in Oxbridge.

Two final points on Oxbridge clothing etiquette must be made. They may seem obvious, but their observation is crucial.

The first concerns university sweatshirts. These are on a par with, or possibly lower than, the crested cufflinks *et al.* described above. It is nothing short of a disgrace that Oxbridge should have sunk to dabbling in the practice of their manufacture, a habit imported to our ordinary universities by their American counterparts. No Oxbrite will *ever* wear an Oxford or Cambridge university sweatshirt or T-shirt. The only circumstances under which they might be worn are these: a genuine Oxford Oxbrite might wear a Cambridge university shirt *after he has come down*, and vice versa. Oxbrites from either university may wear Idontgoto University shirts at any time.

The second is the tying of the bow-tie. Contributors to such magazines as *Harpers and Queen* purport to be alarmed at the thought of a made-up bow-tie; but it is truly said of Oxbrites that they would rather die than wear an elasticated or (worse) a clip-on concoction. Cruel Oxbrites at formal dinner parties (even in the World Outside if the cognac has flowed adequately) will playfully tug at your tie and be genuinely shocked if it does not undo, or comes away whole in their hand. Real bow-ties fit better anyway, and there is nothing to tying them at all. It is just like tying a shoelace. Older Oxbrites even frown at the man who uses a butterfly-ended tie, as opposed to a square-ended one (butterfly ends are supposed to be easier, and are thus Not Cricket). Ignore such censure; it is out of date.

Remember that bow-ties in the World Outside are rare. Only Sir Winston Churchill wore, and Sir Robin Day wears, them with any success. On other people, even Oxbrites, they have an unnerving tendency to make you look either

(a) Armenian, or
(b) like a Wally.

Be cautious of wearing them other than with evening dress.

Half the art of dressing lies in knowing where to shop. At Cambridge, Rose Crescent (known to older Oxbrites as a rather seedy little passage containing one good cheap Italian, a questionable pub and a legendary tobacconist's) has become Incredibly Trendy. *She* will do her more expensive shopping here – at Monsoon, Ferns, Boules and Connections. Connections replaces Bacon's tobacco shop – news which will grieve older Oxbrites, who will remember saving up to buy a packet of 'Calverley' cigarettes. Calverley's 'Ode to Tobacco' remains on its bronze plaque on the wall outside, however.

Classical clothes for men and women are still to be had at Eaden Lilley and at 'Josh Tosh' (Joshua Taylor). Older male Oxbrites will be glad to know that A. & G. Taylor is still in Trinity Street (its window display apparently unchanged in 20 years – but how can tweedy hats date?); as is Roper's, and the excellent Arthur Shepherd.

At Oxford, the doyenne of shops for Her is Annabel-inda. Despite its prices this is Commem. and Summer Ball Mecca to all Oxbrites who are well-heeled enough. A close co-runner is Campus, at 44–5 the High, tantalizingly opposite the Examination Schools.

He will go to the imposing Shepherd and Woodward in the High, opposite Brasenose, for academic and sports wear, or to Castell's (the Broad), Hall's (the Broad) or Walter's (the Turl) for club clothes.

For bespoke tailoring, Oxbrites go to Stamp's (the Broad), and country Oxbrites used to deal with Zacharias (the Corn) before its demise. Watson's Jeans, and Macs-a-Million in the Covered Market will cover every possible Oxbrite leg in jeans.

〚11〛
Social Life I: Societies and clubs – food and booze

OXBRITES ARE NOT a recognizable social type any more. They are drawn increasingly from all walks of life. The moulding process is what makes them Oxbrites, and which confers on them that essential Oxbridge quality which is discernible in people as disparate as a Yorkshire television director and a London barrister. This moulding process is achieved very largely through Oxbridge social life, which is as crucial, if not more so, to the development of the Oxbrite as his *vita academica*.

'You may still be able to tell an Oxford graduate by his command of the absolute position of equilibria, or his unexpected ability to quote the younger Seneca in the context of an income-tax demand: but you could not tell him, as once they say you could, just by the way he walked into a room.'

This statement, if we extend its application from Oxford to Oxbridge, is only partly true, and the third part is unfairly pessimistic, as the following examples show: the first is from 1848; the second from 1968:

' "Perhaps I can read you, Sir, better than you can me. You are an Oxford man by your appearance."

'Charles assented. "How came you," he added, "to suppose I was of Oxford?"

' "Not entirely by your looks and manner," replied the stranger, "for I saw you jump from the omnibus at Steventon; but with that assistance it was impossible to mistake." '

'Clive' was hitching a lift up the A1 back to Cambridge. The event related took place near South Mimms, so there could be no geographical clue to his destination. 'Clive' had been waiting for a long time for a lift, and was getting fed up, so when he saw a sports car approaching, he thumbed with great expression. The car drew up.

> DRIVER: Jump in. I'm going to Cambridge too.
> 'CLIVE': But how . . .?
> DRIVER: I could tell by the way you were hitching.

Thus it is that Oxbrites, particularly when they are 'up', will sometimes go to extraordinary lengths to disguise their place of education, especially when they are travelling in the long vacations, or when they are introduced to Older People Who Are Likely To Be Impressed.

The more general reasons for not admitting to being an Oxbrite derive from:

(a) inverted snobbery
(b) the genuine desire not to advertise one's privilege (see Chapter 10).

The lengths to which Oxbrites have gone to avoid discovery are illustrated by two examples: of the Oxford Oxbrite who pretended to be a Norwegian while travelling in Greece, and the Cambridge Oxbrite who told everybody that, yes, he *was* studying at Cambridge, but as an apprentice for Pye. To no avail. The secret can never be concealed, because the attempt to conceal is *in itself* quintessentially Oxbridge.

It will now be necessary to look at the kind of clubs and societies which shape the Oxbrite. Oxbridge has hundreds of them, at both university and college level, but it is not my intention to review all of them. Full lists can be found in the various Oxbridge handbooks. I intend to avoid discussion of the many worthy academic societies, such as the O.U. Entomological Society, or the C.U. Processor Group and Computer Society. Nor do I intend to do more than mention the several dance, music and art societies and groups which are serious in purpose and available in less rarefied forms even in ordinary universities. I will restrict myself to examining the clubs which the People Who Make Things Happen join – the clubs which spew their products into some of the noisiest positions in the World Outside: those which revolve around entertainment, journalism and politics. As reflections of the Oxbridge mentality, I will also look at *dotty* societies, *grey* societies and dining clubs.

Entertainment means theatre. Outside the dozens of university and college dramatic clubs, a handful dominate at Oxbridge. In this area Cambridge is, and always has been, front runner. The generalization that Oxford produces writers and Cambridge produces actors and directors is true, though don't bandy it about too much among theatrical Oxbrites in the World Outside – on the surface they tend to play down their Cambridge origins, telling you that they only went because they couldn't get into RADA.

Oxford has the Oxford University Dramatic Society, or OUDS, called 'Ouds' by everybody in the know. Together with the ETC, or Experimental Theatre Company, it dominates the theatrical demi-monde. You get in, either as an actor or a director, through a 'Cuppers' competition,[1] organized for freshmen to show how good they are, in the Michaelmas term. OUDS tends to be traditional and classical, producing a 'Major' show only once a term – but for a two-week run. The ETC is more innovative and modern. Their equivalent at Cambridge is to be found in the Amateur Dramatic Club (ADC; founded 1855). This club covers all areas of drama.

[1] Not to be confused with Cambridge 'Cuppers', of course.

Productions for newcomers are rather cruelly called 'Nurseries'; productions for budding directors are called 'Experimentals'. 'Main' productions are presented twice a term or more. The other major drama group which all Oxbrites have heard of is the Marlowe Society, which produces one major Shakespeare or similar play at the Arts Theatre at the end of the Lent term. To perform in this production (until recently the actors were uncredited in the programme but everyone knew who they were) is a sought-after honour. Many knives have entered many backs down the years in pursuit of it. The ADC has its own theatre; the OUDS shares the Oxford Playhouse with a professional company.

In addition to these, Cambridge has the Experimental Theatre *Group* (now called 'European'), a club set up in the late fifties by two undergraduates, Jeremy Leighton and Michael Deakin, to take Shakespeare plays to Europe in the Michaelmas vacation. The classical Greek play is done in February once every three years – in Greek, of course. Some Oxbrites will also remember the Oxford and

Cambridge Shakespeare Company, started in 1969 to take the Bard's plays on tour to America; and in the late sixties Prince Charles brought Trinity's dusty Dryden Society briefly into the limelight by playing the cello and doing skits with dustbins.

The ranks of successful Oxbridge theatricals are not thin: Derek Jacobi, Ian McKellen, Diana Quick and Michael York are good names to drop, and Trevor Nunn and Sir Peter Hall were both at Cambridge. The most ostentatious club for injecting people into the entertainment industry is, however, Cambridge's Footlights.

The Footlights (motto: *ars est celare artem*) is a small club, which twice a term holds smoking concerts or 'smokers', and once a year produces a revue at the Arts Theatre in May Week (George 'Dadie' Rylands sometimes refers to the Arts disparagingly as the 'Town' Theatre, but most Oxbrites get a considerable buzz from working in a *professional* building). Old Oxbrites who were members will remember the termly 'fixture' cards (discontinued on grounds of cost in the seventies), and the clubroom at number 5, Falcon Yard. This place was pulled down in 1974 in the Lion Yard Development behind and including the south side of Petty Cury, but older Oxbrites will remember it with, the author supposes, affection. The uninitiated could be forgiven for wondering why: it shared a rickety building down a dismal alley with the Cruising[1] Club, and as the clubroom was above a fishmonger's the smell was sometimes resistible. The clubroom itself had a number of battered chairs covered in shiny blue or green plastic, small wood-look formica bar tables in the last stages of decay, and an orange and yellow patterned carpet so dirty as to be biologically alive. At one end, on a minute stage with a proscenium decorated with flaking cream paint, participants cavorted to the laughter or

[1] i.e. sailing.

sneers of their fellows in the audience below on the nights of smokers. At the opposite end of the room, a small cream-painted bar dispensed tepid and fizzy beer, and, at lunchtimes, indigestible pie and beans.

At 'smokers', the place was arranged as a tiny theatre, and packed. This was the last bastion of Edwardian gentlemen's music hall (women had only really been *personae gratae* here since Eleanor Bron got things started as early as 1957). Here was the cradle of suspended adolescence which was ultimately responsible for such phenomena as Monty Python and the Goodies. At smokers, members performed sketches and sang songs (selected by audition by the club committee – a power indeed in Cambridge theatreland). You wore a dj if you were a man and your best long velvet number if you were a woman. First-year female would-bes would do little short of kill to be invited to a smoker. Not everyone could just roll up and join Footlights, either. You had to be good to get in!

Footlights was founded in 1883, and in 1885 the remark was first recorded that 'of course, it's nothing like it used to be'. It has survived many changing fashions in humour. Currently it has more in common with its early history than the boom in 'silly' humour in the late fifties and early sixties, and the 'satire' that followed it. Without its Falcon Yard premises, it now rents a room in the Union Society cellars, and its membership is only 80; but its annual revues spawn international tours that have been known to support their organizers in employment for up to a year after coming down from Cambridge.

A list of all the luminaries Footlights has produced would be too long, but as an example of some of the names useful to the Oxbrite or would-be Oxbrite in the pursuit of a media or theatre career, the author offers the following. The student of this book should take especial care to reminisce about people who could be his approximate contemporaries – or he may be found out:

Humphrey Barclay
Lord Bessborough
Michael Billington
Eleanor Bron
Tim Brooke-Taylor
Rob Buckman (who once
said to a fellow Oxbrite
at Footlights, 'Next
time you come, wear
better socks.')
Graham Chapman
John Cleese
Peter Cook
Julie Covington
Russell Davies (a
polymath known as
Dai Davies at
Cambridge)
Jimmy Edwards
Fred Emery

John Fortune
Michael Frayn
David Frost
Graeme Garden
Eric Idle
Clive James
Peter Jeffrey
Lord Killanin
John Lloyd
Graeme McDonald
Jonathan Miller
Trevor Nunn
Bill Oddie
John Pardoe
Jeff Patty
Frederick Raphael
Jan Ravens
Griff Rhys-Jones
Julian Slade
Ian Wallace

... and these are just a few. A study of this list, and a
comparison of how the people on it are placed, and in
what relation to each other, in the World Outside, is
rewardingly interesting. It is interesting, too, that
Jonathan Miller is on it, since he has been quoted as
saying, 'I can hardly remember anything about theatre in
Cambridge. It played a very small part in my life. I wasn't
a member of either Footlights or the ADC.' John Cleese
remembers: 'I spent a lot of my last two years in the
Footlights Club, almost entirely because I enjoyed the
company so much. In the early sixties, no one even
considered the possibility of a career in show business. I
remember too that we were rather in awe of the proper
actors, who wore jeans and black leather jackets and
talked about motivation and Brecht. Someone a bit like

LUMINARY

this directed me in my first revue. But he supported Ipswich Town and was really quite nice. His name was Trevor Nunn. I always wondered what happened to him.' Later sixties Oxbrites will remember the patriarchal figure of Clive James, usually clad in a brown leather bomber jacket, apparently rooted to a stool in the bar corner of the clubroom.

Where Cambridge has the Footlights, Oxford has the aptly named Etceteras.

A word on film must be given before I leave the area of entertainment. Many Oxbrites *live* in the cinema, lapping up every genre director from Pabst to Bergman, and occasionally having fun with grockle-movies. Thus an Oxbrite was once thrown out of the Victoria cinema, Cambridge, for standing on his seat and cheering when

Julie Andrews is cornered by the Gestapo in *The Sound of Music*. At Cambridge, too, in the fifties, a group of undergraduates dressed as priests and attended a screening of *The Ten Commandments*, during which they passed loud, irreverent comments. No one dared eject *them*.

Serious Cambridge film-goers used to have a number of cinemas to choose from, but now that the Rex (where Leslie Halliwell, as the cinema's manager, made sure that Cambridge was the first town in Britain to be hit by *The Wild One*) and the Kinema are no more, only the Arts Cinema in Arts Passage remains. The university film society is still going strong (Oxbrites in their mid-thirties will remember Sunday evening screenings in Lady Mitchell Hall under the presidencies of David Hare and Tony Rayns), and most colleges have a film club too. The town still has the Victoria in Market Hill, and the Regal in Regent Street is now an ABC. Both these house more than one cinema these days. Oxbridge film buffs should *not* be fooled by the society called: 'People Who Have Seen John Wayne As A Roman Centurion Say "Truly This Man Was The Son Of God" In *The Greatest Story Ever Told*'.

At Oxford, the principal 'art' cinemas are the Moulin Rouge, miles away in Headington High Street, and the Phoenix in Walton Street. Ascetics on a budget tramp to the Penultimate Picture Palace in faraway Jeune Street – though the PPP has all the advantages of being a cinema club. There are ABCs in George Street and Magdalen Street. Older Oxbrites will remember endless late-night Marx brothers sessions at the Central (Cambridge; now a bingo hall), and the end-of-term Ealing Comedy at the Moulin – usually *Kind Hearts and Coronets*.

Film-making goes on at Oxbridge, too. Cambridge lags rather in this respect, but the relatively recent Oxford Film Foundation has already put out one feature film – the underwhelming *Privileged* – and plans another.

* * *

Older Cambridge Oxbrites will no doubt be horrified to learn of the demise of *Varsity* – the university's principal weekly newspaper – in 1973. *Varsity*, founded in 1931, and which numbered among its editors such unlikely people as Michael Winner, gave way after 42 years of trivia to *Stop Press*, which not only takes itself rather more seriously (its journalists regularly picking up *Guardian* Student Journalist awards), but is distributed free to colleges. Similarly the left-wing *1/– Paper* of the late sixties has given way to *The Heckler*, not unlike it in format, but subject to all the difficulties of persuading a mainly though mildly right-wing 'public' to interest itself in left-wing ideas. The arts review *Broadsheet* survives, but its present reputation for levity would shock more serious journalists, such as Hugh Pile, who ran it fifteen years ago (Pile, now Editor of LWT's *Weekend World*, played First Groom in the Marlowe Society's 1970 production of *Henry IV* Part 2). Further upmarket, and away from the undergraduates, dons will read *The Cambridge Review*; and *Granta* is now a literary journal published by Penguin, and far removed from its origins as an undergraduate magazine.

At Oxford, the weekly rag is called *Cherwell*, which takes itself less seriously than *Stop Press*, and tends to be even more jejeune, but is more fun. *Isis* is a fortnightly features magazine which has numbered among its contributors and editors such a varied bunch of people as Anthony Holden, Gyles Brandreth and James Fenton. The third major magazine, *Tributary*, will only be known to younger Oxbrites (post 1975), and specializes in childish satire. Older Oxbrites will remember the poetry magazine *Carcanet* – now grown into a poetry publishing house of repute.

If budding politicians are not cutting their teeth with the journalists, they will be sounding off with the collection of invited bores, has-beens and drones from the World Outside who infest the Oxbridge Union Societies.

The Union Societies, usually just called the Unions, are, of course, nothing to do with the Students' Unions: they are debating societies which supposedly nurture tomorrow's men and women of influence. Oxford Oxbrites constantly remind you that the Oxford Union is better than the Cambridge one. This they do on the strength of the notoriety of the 1933 debate, 'This House Would Not Fight For King And Country', although to be fair the Union also boasts Gladstone, Michael Foot and Tariq Ali among its former presidents. Cambridge can field two distinguished former women presidents: Ann Mallalieu (1967), now a barrister, who was recently able to get tax relief on clothing costs for those in her profession, and Arianna Stassinopoulos (1971), the Greek writer and personality. Women weren't actually allowed to join until 1963.

The truth is that the unions are beginning to totter. Their stature has dwindled mightily since their days of real glory (1880–1930), maintenance costs force their membership fees higher than most undergraduates are prepared to pay, and, worst of all, they are beginning to be thought *out*. However, as mini Houses of Commons (with all the attendant intrigue) they are still useful for those making a bid for the dustier corners of that world. For older Oxbrites the picture is a bit different, but on the whole anyone now under 40 will be inclined to go vague when asked if he ever spoke at the Union. Advantages include free snooker, quite good bars and cheaply-hireable rooms for parties.

It is not my purpose to discuss straightforward political societies in general, but comments from male Oxbrites have included: 'Liberal women are OK as long as they don't open their mouths; Labour women are earnest and plain, and won't shut up; Tory women are OK for a steady income.' The Oxford Humanist Society is remembered for having 'the prettiest women with a liberal outlook' – thus proving that sex is still a greater dynamic than politics, or even moral reform.

A word of warning about all three principal groups described above: the newcomer will find them peopled with Oxbrites who take life far too seriously and who are, in general, fretfully ambitious and insecure. They will do their best at all times to humiliate you and make you feel that you have about as much talent as a dead rat. Do not be put off: this is all excellent training for *life*, and Oxbrites in the World Outside frequently blather on about how their ability to rise above such things at Oxbridge gave them the courage/grit to get where they are today. The chances are that when they were 'up' they were just as bad as everyone else. In any case all three areas of activity are regarded by younger Oxbrites as *out*.

Dotty societies often sound like fun, but be careful in your selection, as they can be the haunt of the grey man, gnome or bore. They can also simply be disorganized drinking clubs. Among the better ones at Cambridge are:

The Dampers' Club: this is described as a sporting and social club open only to those who have 'entered the river Cam unwillingly from a punt while fully clothed'. So far so good. But the club lists its activities as underwater cycle racing, punt jousting, poohsticks and underwater punt racing, so do not admit membership of it if you have any desire at all to be thought sophisticated. The May Ball Appreciation Society (see more, below) exists for people who are 'interested in flouting the most stringent security surrounding certain large events occurring in the middle of June'. As training, equipment (e.g. scaling ladders) and techniques are provided, and as May Balls have always cost the earth, this society sounds promising, but I suspect not for ladies who are not also hearties, since gatecrashing

underwater punt racing

over a flint wall from a punt in a £200 ball gown is not everyone's idea of fun. Probably the best bet in this category at Cambridge is the CUMWC – the Cambridge University Mud Wrestling Club, which speaks for itself, though less energetic Oxbrites will prefer the Strawberry Society.

Intrepid clubs include the one which goes in for 'night-climbing' – a pastime which involves crossing Cambridge by a series of routes which are mapped out along the roofs of the various colleges. The circuit of Trinity Great Court has not yet been successfully completed, so don't say that you've done it. The Colonial Feethounds of the fifties existed to throw Trinity beagles (and beaglers) into the Cam.

At Oxford there have been The Society For Photographing Dons In Bed, and The Society For Stealing Taps From College Bathrooms, but most of the lunatic fringe societies there come under the guise of dining clubs. This, and the fact that membership is nearly always by invitation only, is another example of how much more old-fashioned Oxford is than Cambridge. Before we pass on to dining clubs, however, a general warning note must briefly be sounded on *grey* societies: avoid anything which involves board games, Morris dancing or Hobbits.

Dining clubs exist at all levels, and only a selection can be offered here. One or two drinking clubs are included as well.

Cambridge is restrained. Perfectly respectable societies exist, such as the King's Wine and Food Society, and the C.U. Wine Society; these are serious in purpose and their members would be shocked if you suggested that they were merely a good excuse for a debauch. More fun exists on a college level, and it is heartening to see that even such a modern college as Robinson already has a Real Gin Society, and a Crusoe Dinner at which the statutory drinking per person is: half a bottle of sherry; four bottles of wine; half a bottle of port; brandy (as much as you can). Another 'new' college, Churchill, is the home of the Penguin Club. Membership is by invitation only, and limited to 150 at a time. Since membership is free, a nucleus of members (there are five of them) supply the booze. The annual party is in the Lent term, and the invitation reads: 'To Celebrate the Melting of the Pack Ice and the Beginning of the Mating Season'. At the party, you 'mate' with somebody by passing a mint imperial from mouth to mouth, and dress (unisex) is dinner jacket and shorts. More sophisticated clubs include Queens' College Silver Boars, but probably the doyen of Cambridge decadence is the Wyley Society of Magdalene.

This holds, at various times throughout the year, a Tasting and a Cricket Match (at which the position of square leg umpire was once taken by a crate of beer), but *the* event in its calendar is the Drinks Party. This takes place in the form of an At Home in the Magdalene Fellows' Garden in May Week. The society is run by the 'trustees', and the black-edged invitation cards read, 'The Executors of the late Sir Joshua Wyley . . .'. There are 25 trustees, and the host-executors shell out about £75 each for the booze. Two hundred people are invited, and to be invited imparts great prestige to the guest. There are, however, dangers.

The basic drink, horribly enough, is grapefruit juice and vodka. If an executor requests you to drink, you may not refuse, and what is more, you have to 'bumper' your glass – i.e. drink it off in one; and you have to drink in this way as many glasses as you are requested to. A variation of this is 'bumper races'[1] – at which the loser has to drink another. In 1980 all three emergency services were called, and an unpleasant rumour suggested that the Master's

---

[1] Not to be confused with 'Bumps' – see below.

daughter lost her virginity. Departing guests have been so sloshed that they have mistaken police cars for taxis, and once one man's heart stopped. He recovered from the subsequent coma three days later in Addenbrooke's, and his first action was to call for a drink.

How much more refined seems the atmosphere suggested by the invitation to the King's annual cricket match between the Choir and the Gentlemen: 'You are invited to act as a scorer on the occasion of a cricket match between the Gentlemen of King's and the Choral Scholars ... Sartorial Elegance, and a General Sense of the Occasion, are the only necessary qualifications.'

Before leaving Cambridge, there are two more clubs to which we must make reference. The Pitt Club, bastion of the ultra-right, is to be found in Jesus Lane, just round the corner from the ADC. Built as a swimming pool in 1863 by the Roman Bath Company Ltd, its crumbling façade reflects its ailing fortunes, little helped by leasing its former dining room to a swish restaurant and cocktail bar called, of all things, Xanadu. (This will be news to older Oxbrites.) Xanadu's kitchens also cater for Pitt Clubbers (though where *they* eat now is a mystery). One of the least likely former members of the club is Salman Rushdie – for most of them were so high Tory that in 1970 they refused even to vote for Heath (What? Vote for Heath, the Bugger?), and none would have voted for a lower-middle-class Chemistry graduate from Somerville nine years later, however brilliantly she led the country.

The second is the Apostles, a secret society of dons and undergraduates who gather together on account of their superior intellects. They see themselves as the *crème de la crème*, and membership, by secret invitation only, is greatly coveted. You can't even tell outsiders who else is in it. Historic Apostles (the club was founded in 1820) include Tennyson, Lytton Strachey and Guy Burgess.

It is to Oxford that we must look, though, for the *vraie*

chose when it comes to dining clubs. Older Oxbrites may reminisce about them with pride, disgust or awe, according to which club is in question. Younger Oxbrites should take note that dining societies are a relic of a former age (indeed, they have been that for 30 years), although some of them remain obstinately *in*.

The Assassins, then, is run by a group of 'officers' who call themselves the Junta. The club organizes a large drinks party once a term, and various dinners are held *ad hoc*.[1] There are only about 20 members at a time, so the would-be Oxbrite claiming to have been an Assassin should take care; his claim may be verifiable. Politically right-wing, but not snobbish about 'new' money, the Assassins gained typical notoriety a few years ago when, in the especial company of one of their number, the heir to a well-known firm of grocers, they completely destroyed a restaurant just outside Oxford.

A more establishment club is the expensive and exclusive Bullingdon, founded 150 years ago, mentioned in Waugh (but not in dispatches) and originally owing its *raison d'être* to hunting. Membership is by election, like the Assassins, and like the Assassins the Bullingdon is nowadays considered too old hat to be anything but *out*, though older Oxbrites who move in stodgy circles (big wheels in local government) may raise a snigger by alluding to it.

Another sporting club which older Oxbrites will enjoy talking about is Vincent's, exclusive to Blues (see more, below), with its set of upper rooms off the High; but the most famous Tory dining club is the Gridiron, in Shoe Lane. The 'Grid' will even provide useful contacts for the World Outside in areas such as the Law, Politics and Industry. More endearing are the Dinosaurs (New College), whose members each assume the name of a dinosaur (my informant was Elasmosaurus), and the Pat-

[1] No pun intended.

riarchs, whose members take the names of Roman senators or patricians, and who dine in maroon bow-ties, with matching maroon lapels to their silk waistcoats. Last but not least of the principal élitist clubs is the Piers Gaveston, for the glamorous, rich and self-consciously decadent – and open to women, though *all* members are elected. This one is a bit of a strain but it was still *in* at the time of writing. Older Oxbrites be warned: it has been founded since your time: do not claim to have been a member.

Before leaving this section, some mention should be made of The Queen's College Piglets, rare among dining clubs in having a liberal outlook and freely admitting women; and the Guttersnipes, which 'devotes its energy to wining and dining in unusual, dangerous or remote places'.

Oxford dining clubs should be applauded for remaining, by and large, firmly reactionary amid the wash of liberalism which surrounds them nowadays. Oxbrites who are not elected to, or who have no interest in, any such societies must seek their food and booze elsewhere. If you are one such, do not give up hope. You are one of many. One of the key Oxbridge myths is that you have to join a club to have fun. This is the *last* reason why most people join clubs. They join them rather to get on, and to be thought well of.

Older Cambridge Oxbrites will be sorry, but possibly not surprised to learn that M. André and his Le Jardin are things of the past. Once one of the most expensive restaurants in town (at a heady £3 per person in 1967), and one of the best French restaurants in the country, it has now gone with the *neiges d'antan*. The Coffee Pot in Green Street has been replaced by the Oasis, a modestly Arab foray into the cheap restaurant circuit in Cambridge, which is generally controlled by Greeks. The Whim in Trinity Street survives; those who remember it as a charming place for tea either have defective memories, or are inexcusably sentimental, for it was never that; but now – horror of horrors! – it has become a *hamburger joint*!! Another, earlier metamorphosis (*c.* 1969) has overtaken the Gardenia, which survives in name only in Rose Crescent. Once shabbily-genteel Italian, it is now brash Greek. The Friar House opposite the Eagle in Bene't Street also retains its name – but it is now a curio shop. The Bistro Italo in Northampton Street – which opened in the late sixties to great acclaim on account of its trendy décor, huge helpings and reasonable prices, has been replaced by something called Crusts. Crusts, I am told, is where Magdalene men like taking language school women to impress them.

It will come as a relief to older Oxbrites to know that the Arts Theatre Restaurant (the Pentagon) remains *unchanged to the last detail*, as does the Arts' Roof Garden Buffet, still serving cheap (£1.85) steak and kidney pie, soggy chips and tinned peas, which you can wash down in the stifling heat with a pint of tepid and fizzy keg beer from the bar. In Bridge Street, the Bombay is one of the few Indian survivors from 25 years ago.

Younger Oxbrites are more aware of the Greek brigade: two Eros restaurants – the one in St John's Street bad; the one in the Petty Cury shopping centre good, and constantly remembered; and the Eraina doles out the usual 'moussaka-and-potatoes-with-a-bottle-of-retsina-or-if-you-prefer-what-about-kleftiko?' stuff. Special occasion Oxbrites go to Don Pasquale's, a basement Italian on Market Hill,[1] and those with transport will use the Old Fire Engine House at Ely; the Pink Geranium at Melbourn is good for people with deep pockets, a taste for chintz and a sweet tooth.

Oxford has the nice-looking but disappointing Mitre in

[1] 'Hill' in flat Cambridge means 'open space'.

the High. Best known and priciest in town are (1) the Elizabeth in St Aldate's, opposite to Christ Church's Meadow Gate and next door to Lewis Carroll's 'Old Sheep Shop'; and (2) La Sorbonne in the High, very French and very dear, but worth it. Neither of these is really within the range of undergraduate pockets, however, and Oxbrites should reminisce about them with caution – especially if they are not, or were not, rich. Younger Oxbrites speak fondly of Michel's Brasserie in Little Clarendon Street (the street incidentally, where women undergraduates, who call it 'Little Trendy Street', will find their day wear, and where Habitatty shops like Usborne's will part with knick-knacks to brighten your rooms).

Italian restaurants are legion, but best loved and most affectionately remembered of Oxbrites since the early sixties are La Cantina in Queen Street, the Luna Caprese in North Parade and the Saraceno in Magdalen Street. Because Oxford is more opulent than Cambridge, there are many more significant restaurants than can be mentioned here, but the reminiscing Oxbrite should be warned that Brown's in the Woodstock Road has become *too* popular and is now *out* (partly because you always have to queue to get in; partly because the game pie is bony). Brown's should not of course be confused with Brown's (in the Covered Market) which has declined and is now *out* too – although it is lovingly remembered by fifties and sixties Oxbrites for its white tablecloths, milky-coloured crockery and Camp coffee. George's in the Covered Market, and Georgina's upstairs, retain their popularity. Older Oxbrites say that George's is not what it used to be, but it does still seem possible to compete with your fellow diners to build up the largest possible breakfast on your plate (an early sixties winner spent 10s. – at 6d. an item).

Out of town eating for Oxford Oxbrites includes possibilities at the Bear at Woodstock, the Rose Revived at

Newbridge Standlake; and two White Harts – one at Fyfield and one at Wytham (pronounced, of course, White-Ham). Although neither of the last two is renowned for its service, all of the last three are happily remembered. Mainly English cuisine.

All undergraduates and many poorer Oxbrites in the World Outside subsist almost entirely on Indian or Chinese food when they 'go out' to a restaurant. Both Oxford and Cambridge have a plethora of both, but Oxbrites go oddly vague when asked to remember which they ate at. You may like to be armed with the knowledge that at Cambridge the Peking restaurant in Burleigh Street enjoys Ronay's imprimatur, and that in Oxford the place to go for 'Indos' is Walton Street. Self-catering Cambridge Oxbrites will be sad to learn that the Dorothy supermarket has gone, but as man cannot live by bread alone they will be relieved that Jarrold's is still there, purveying ream upon ream of narrow feint and students' notebooks for those who put their brains above their bellies. Self-catering Oxford Oxbrites of 40+, by the way, should be aware of the demise of Brimley and Hughes in the mid-sixties.

A final point to remember is that it is generally considered *out* to insult the staff in restaurants these days – although certain hearty Oxbrites still enjoy confusing waiters who have a poor grasp of English. Younger Oxbrites consider it bad form to upset the menials – in any case, restaurants are so expensive today that one is humbled by the prices. Making a good deal of noise and mess is also felt to be *out* these days – for similar reasons.

The principal beers available in Cambridge are Tolly and Greene King, but a more important distinction lies in which pub is Town and which is Gown – a distinction which is less clear at Oxford.

Queens' men will remember The Anchor, a place of spartan décor and uninspired architecture redeemed by its closeness to the river, and its convenience for punt hiring facilities. At the other end of town, the Fort St George on Victoria Avenue by the Cam is full of boaties, but has the advantage of being open all day during Bumps, and male Oxbrites remember it as a place where you could quite often run into very attractive colonial girls on their grand tour of the Old Country. The Mitre in Bridge Street was once a nonentity but is now full of Stop Press hacks, and at the nearby Baron of Beef dullness is overcome by convenience from the point of view of John's hearties and choral scholars. The Eagle, with its inn-yard and good cold lunch buffet, is remembered with more fondness by older than younger Oxbrites, since in recent years it has been discovered and taken over by tourists. The Bath Hotel next door, once the haunt of the flat cap, sports jacket and cavalry twill brigade, is now exclusively Townie. Some young Oxbrites have barely even heard of it. Also, the Rose in Rose Crescent, scene of many a seedy literary lunch, has been replaced by a wine bar called Flambard's. All that remains of the Rose is the cast-iron lamp bracket. Be warned.

In the days before the wine bar became the basis of sophistication, Miller's Wine Parlour stood at the corner of King's Parade and Bene't Street. Really *soigné* Oxbrites would repair there for glasses of hock and thin duck pâté sandwiches until 1971, when, in a move which should have called thunderbolts down on the heads of the perpetrators, it was closed down. From its ashes arose a wine bar called Shades – much beloved, alas, of seventies and eighties male Oxbrites who don't know any better, who think the place trendy and who welcome the opportunity of chatting up foreign language school women which its gloom affords.

At Oxford, the dominating beers are Hall's, Morrell's and Morland's. In the centre of town, Oxbrites will remember the tiny Bear with mixed feelings. Walls and

ceiling are covered with glass cases containing moulder-
ing snippets of various club and school ties. The collection
transcends Oxford, and is said to be the greatest of its kind
in the world, which no one would find hard to believe.
Patrons tend to be Christ Church men and Oriel ruggerbuggers. The Eagle and Child in St Giles' (known to
Oxbrites variously as the Bird and Babe, Bird and Bastard and even the Fowl and Foetus) used to be a haunt of
Tolkien and C. S. Lewis, but it's looked down upon these
days. Across the road, the Lamb and Flag looks like the
Genuine Article from the outside, but inside it's all tiles
and blaring video juke-boxes. Younger Oxbrites with a
liberal outlook enjoy it because of the opportunity it
affords of mingling with the common ruck of humanity.
Male Oxbrites like St Giles' pubs because of the opportunity they provide of bumping into nurses from the Radcliffe Infirmary.

The King's Arms, known as the KA, was for many
years the place for OUDS people to go, and one older
Oxbrite remembers one day when Diana Quick held court
there, 'showing her admirers her belly-button'. The
Chequers and the Wheatsheaf, both off the High, were for
a long time considered havens from one's fellow Oxbrites
– although in practice so many of one's fellow Oxbrites
thought so too that the objective was self-defeating. Older
Oxbrites may remember them with affection.

The Turf is a little Free House with two gardens and
food which has been mentioned in Egon Ronay. It is thus
always full, but remains attractive and popular. The
White Horse next door to Blackwell's is a Trinity pub. It
has a lovingly kept shove-ha'penny board; and do not be
put off by the myriad sporting photographs on the walls: it
is not over-hearty, and its Hall's is very drinkable.

Another favourite, particularly with sixties and seventies Oxbrites, is the Vicky (Victoria) Arms, on the river
Cherwell just north of the Marston Ferry Road. The

〚12〛

Social Life II: Balls, parties and sex

WHEN OXBRITES are not consuming alcohol, they are consuming equally large quantities of tea and *instant* coffee. The latter drink, which of course is completely different from coffee, is drunk in great quantities while working, and especially when doing 'all-nighters' (see Glossary); but it is not essentially a social drink (except among grey men).

'Tea (the meal not the drink) was the great mating ritual,' remembers a late fifties vintage Oxbrite, and although in his day it was at the now sadly defunct Fuller's in Oxford that one went to meet a potential mate, tea remains a social occasion at Oxbridge which it has long ceased to be elsewhere. So strong is the influence of tea on the Oxbridge mind that some Oxbrites in the World Outside will still invite you to tea and think it nothing strange not to offer you alcohol at all.

Why tea? In a word, because it's cheaper than booze. Of course, if one is hell-bent on seduction it's not quite as effective, but Oxbrites like to keep their options open and so the gentility of the tea party provides an ideal arena for them to stalk each other in, and one in which the subtlest signals can be exchanged. A Cambridge undergraduate, for example, could be pretty sure of success if the male of her choice bought her cakes from Fitzbillie's for tea. The tea party need not be the exclusive preserve of sexual socializing, either. It only takes two friends and a bag full of crumpets to make a tea party. At one such 'crumpet

the great mating ritual

orgy', two Oxbrites ate 30 crumpets in two hours. Tea is useful, too, for filling up the dead hours between lunch and opening time.

Parties which do not adumbrate moves in the sex game, but which provide a useful forum for meeting New People, are those of the Sherry and Cocktail variety. These are at their best on lawns in summer, and preferably given by dons who can afford good quality drink, and whose example *usually* minimizes the risk of the whole thing degenerating into an orgy. The word 'party' covers a multitude of sins at Oxbridge. In the bad old days when the ratio of women to men was about 1:10, an Oxbrite remembers going to a party in someone's rooms, where about twenty desperate men were drinking cheap wine from pint glasses and showing off unbearably to two fresher women undergraduates, too green to handle the situation and now pressed despairingly into a corner. He does not remember their fate, since the pints of Spanish Sauternes got to him long before the end of the party and he had to dive off into the sanctuary of a friendly rhododendron in the court outside. In the early sixties Pimm's parties were still affordable, and one of our informants remembers a happy occasion at such a party when he heard two other Oxbrites bitching about him – too drunk to be aware that he was standing next to them.

Colleges tend to have good cellars, and drink flows freely. For freshers this can be a terrifying experience, especially if they are given to timidity, or come from one of the more backward of the English provinces. 'I'd never been to a sherry party before – I didn't know what to do,' moaned one, ostracized for dunking her biscuit.

Party-going does not become enjoyable until your second year, by which time you will have clawed your way into some kind of position in society; but party-going has one important side-effect, the social significance of which cannot be underestimated. I refer to the Invitation.

Oxbrites are generally not on the telephone when they are 'up', especially if they live in rooms. They communicate with each other by means of notes sent through the (free) internal postal systems of the universities, or popped personally under doors. Those letters and notes delivered via the post find their destination in 'pigeonholes' by the porters' lodge of each college. Oxbrites eagerly ransack their pigeonholes daily. Freshers get masses of stuff – mainly circulars from obscure religious societies, but including their first Invitations, perhaps to a sherry party with their tutor (moral tutor). As time passes, the Invitations, and the number of them you can display on your chimney-piece,[1] become paramount in importance. The satisfaction an Oxbrite derives from friends' envy at the sight of a full chimney-piece is better imagined than described.

The high point of Oxbridge social life, at least in theory, is the Ball.

The Ball takes place in summer, usually early in June, when most of the exams are over (except for some scientists', and they don't count anyway). Oxford doesn't bestow a specific name on the first two weeks of June (generally the time of post-academic jubilation), but Cambridge, with the typical perversity which the astute student of this book will by now be coming to recognize, calls them *May Week*. This time is one of concentrated party-going, alfresco lunches, open-air plays, punting, and, the jewel in the crown, Balls.

At Cambridge they are called May Balls and most colleges give them annually. Men wear black tie and women wear ball gowns. They cost far too much and most male Oxbrites can only afford to go to one in their three-year career, since Balls are still a bastion of masculinity, in that men invite, and pay for, women to accompany them. Once there, the price of your double ticket (currently averaging £60) generally entitles you to a buffet supper (quality varies with college, but at Cambridge Pembroke generally wins the palm) and a limited amount to drink. The rest you pay for. May Balls run from about 10 p.m. to 6 a.m., when at Cambridge you then traditionally punt a few miles upstream to Grantchester where you have strawberries and champagne for breakfast at the Orchard (otherwise famous for its teas and 'Is There Honey ...'). Magdalene and Pembroke only have May Balls every other year, but they alternate with each other. Their balls are proportion-

[1] The chimney-piece is a crucial item in the furniture of Oxbridge rooms; it exists principally to display Invitations on.

ately grander and more expensive, and at Magdalene, not entirely surprisingly, the men wear white tie.

Oxford balls are organized in a less predictable way. The grand Commemoration Ball, loosely celebrating the college's Foundation, and usually referred to as a 'Commem. Ball', is not held every year, but once every three years or so (depending on the college). A smaller Summer Ball is held annually in the years when there is no Commem.

All Oxbrites are invited to their college ball, even when they have left to join the World Outside – provided that they can stump up for the ticket. But be warned: there can be few sights more miserable than a gaggle of older Oxbrites who have ignored the passage of time and the maxim, 'Never Go Back', huddled at 3 a.m. in a corner of a college court, in the company of bored, cold or peevish non-Oxbrite spouses, thinking of the drive back to London, and fighting off sleep.

I cannot stress enough that, more important than the groups that are playing, the food, or the wine, is the Partner. Feminists may gnash their teeth, but the fact is that most women (especially non-Oxbrites) would do anything short of murder to get an invitation (unless they are older or wiser, or have been to a ball before). Male Oxbrites capitalize on this, but you're still regarded as a bit of a social leper if you're reduced to importing a woman from London, or your home town (or even, at Cambridge, to bringing a non-undergraduate). In the rush to give and receive invitations, any pretence at rationality in the pairing-off process is thrown to the winds, and unless the couple going to the ball is:

(a) established,
(b) happy, and
(c) going in the congenial company of at least one other similar couple,

you have a recipe for disaster, since the very price you are paying induces you to approach the whole question of having a good time with a certain tension.

One anecdote (quite typical) will suffice as a caveat to both sexes. It befell 'Aloysius' at Oxford:

At school, a bare two or three years earlier, 'Aloysius' had loved 'Sheila' from a hopeless distance. Shortly before the Oriel Commem. Ball, for which he had already bought a ticket, he was dumped by his current girlfriend. It was too late to find another at Oxford, and so he quickly wrote to 'Sheila' and invited her. He got a letter by return accepting the invitation and telling him what train to meet.

'The first impression was bad enough,' he recalls today, still blanching at the memory. 'She had put on a ton of weight: she was as wide as the Mersey Tunnel.' But worse was to come. He managed to smuggle her into his rooms unseen by his friends. She retired to the bedroom to change – he closing the door despite all her protests that as they were old friends it did not matter. When she emerged, the next ten hours suddenly stretched before his eyes like a life sentence. She was wearing 'a ball gown that reminded me in girth of the Berlin Wall, only it was in powder blue taffeta edged with pink'. With a heavy heart he took her suitcase back to the hotel he had booked for her.

What could he do? He took her to the ball. But the only way to escape the derision of his friends in the Inner Gobbley Circle (more on this below) was through drink.

It is a feature of balls to screen films during them. 'Aloysius' enticed 'Sheila' into a showing of *Jules et Jim*, and, once she was ensconced in front of the screen, he slipped away to his rooms. It was 2 a.m., the drink had made him tired, and he felt that he could better face the remainder of the night fortified with half an hour's sleep.

He awoke at 3 p.m. the following day. 'Sheila' had

gone. 'And I never saw her again. It was a schoolboy dream shattered.'

Girls tend to go to more balls than men, because:

(a) they don't have to pay, and
(b) it is easier to 'crash' a ball for a girl.

The high cost of balls encourages crashing, and it has been developed into a fine art. If you have friends who run an undergraduate disco which has been hired for the ball then sometimes you can get in with them as 'part of the team'. Occasionally performers in undergraduate drama productions which have been called for to fill a corner at a ball can slip a friend in too. A favoured method in the days before security became tight was to buy a ticket, go in legitimately, establish your identity with the gate porter as the holder of a bona fide ticket, then leave the ball after a while and pass it on to a friend, with whom you had shared the cost. You would then return, having 'lost' your ticket, but the gate porter would recognize you and let you through. Or your 'pass-out' might have been an indelible ink mark placed on your hand by the porter, so there would be no need to produce your ticket again. One Oxbrite informs me that at Cambridge an invisible mark was placed on ballgoers' hands, only detectable by an infra-red scanner, but the likelihood of the truth of this seems to me slight, despite the device's being *very* Cambridge (scientific and unnecessarily complex).

A simpler method of illegal entry is only possible if you are going to a ball in a college where you also have access to rooms. In this case you simply arrive early in the afternoon and stay put in the rooms, emerging, changed into your glad-rags, at about midnight. You then move straight from the staircase entrance into the revelry.

Some balls – the most expensive – are virtually uncrashable, the organizers going these days to unfair lengths of security, such as barbed wire and even alsatian dogs. The

147

romantic way to crash balls, though, is by punt, and this is only possible at Cambridge, because at Oxford only one college (Magdalen) is built by a river. One attempt that worked well took place at the Trinity May Ball of 1973.

The whole secret of the sub-industry of crashing balls is Bide Your Time (though this is not often popular with the more unsporting kind of girl, who sees no fun in hanging around in the cold until it's 1 a.m. and the best groups are over, and then having to climb from a punt over a wall in a ball gown). Waiting is important because after two or three hours the security men and/or porters will have either:

(a) relaxed
(b) become sleepy
(c) ceased to care
(d) got drunk themselves.

This is your cue to punt alongside (with muffled pole) the river wall of the college of the ball of your choice, make fast and climb in.

On this occasion the punter was swept off the punt by a low branch, and, with a hollow cry and a loud splash, disappeared into the darkness. In true Oxbridge fashion[1] the other crashers paid no more attention to him, but scaled the wall and got into the ball, with complete success. A little later they heard a commotion near where their punt was moored. A group of legitimate ballgoers had found it, and decided to borrow it to go for a sail. However, they'd been caught getting into it by security men who thought they were crashers getting *out* of it, and who were now trying to eject them, having been tipped off that there were gatecrashers afoot!

*   *   *

[1] 'The only reason an Oxbrite would ever offer a drowning man a straw would be to see if the proverb were true, that drowning men clutch at them.'

Balls usually provide every possible kind of music, to listen to and dance to, but however good it is, it is immaterial to most true Oxbrites, who, from their late teens on, prefer drinking and talking too much to almost any other activity. What to talk about is something which we must consider. Ancient Oxbrites will be quite happy with general reminiscences, and if you are younger than they are just let them ramble on, occasionally feeding them with lines like, 'Gosh, *really?*' and 'Did you actually manage to do *that?*' This will get most of them eating out of your hand, but if confronted with one whose brain is still functioning, disagree with him now and then to flatter him into thinking he's still considered worthy of arguing with, but always do this respectfully, and always choose unimportant issues, so that he won't bother to pursue them. Judging the degree of unimportance is a fine art, and depends on your Oxbrite. One who can let go the proposition that Hitler Was Misunderstood can get very heated about the quality of college sherry in 1932. Middle-aged Oxbrites will tend to be happy with Politics, or What They Can Remember Of The Subject They Read, if they have been successful in life; or the State Of The World, if they have not.

The easiest Oxbrite to win over to your side is the completely successful one in the World Outside, for once he has accepted that you are an Oxbrite too, and therefore accepted *you*, he will go on to talk about other things. Beware, though, of beady and very precise questions designed to trap you. You should be able to answer, 'Let's see, did you know any Somerville *men?*', but some questions are so complex as to be self-defeating. If asked, 'Isn't there a stuffed owl over the chimney-piece in the inner bar of the Bird and Bastard?', you can answer with perfect *sang-froid* that you don't remember.

General conversation can often be geared to the prevailing fashions of the times. Sixties Oxbrites will know about

Bob Dylan, and the Yardbirds, and about Arrabal and Chomsky, for example. Fifties Oxbrites will be happy with the MJQ, the Dutch Swing College, curry and pipe-smoking. Seventies Oxbrites will give you a lot of guff about 'living at the tail end of the sixties'. Never forget that you will be all right provided that you are not a contemporary of your interlocutor – all you will have to do in such a case is sound intelligent, and if possible mention a couple of their well-known contemporaries in a know-ledgeable way.

If in doubt, or if for any reason you feel cornered, bring the conversation round to sex.

Sex, of course, is the common currency of most conversa-tion, in one guise or another, but at the Oxbridge level it acquires a special intensity. This is because there has always been a great imbalance of the sexes at Oxbridge, thus transforming sex from something natural to be taken in one's stride, to a difficult and even frightening entity, at its worst the object of obsessive analysis.

Although both sexes suffer from this, it is of course men who are to blame. Although in pre-Reformation days the administration of the two all-male universities recognized the need for a natural outlet for the sex drive, and reg-ulated brothels in the towns, by the nineteenth century the search for, and expulsion of, 'common women' had be-come one of the chief duties of the proctors, although a report of the Syndicate of the Town of Cambridge dated 6 March 1854 said nervously: '... we cannot ... refrain from suggesting a doubt whether duties of this kind are strictly compatible with the clerical character, and the Proctors are ... with few exceptions, clergymen.' Proc-torial attempts to control and curb the natural inclina-tions of undergraduates sometimes led them into water too deep for them. On one occasion an Oxbrite was 'prog-ged' in the company of a well-known local prostitute.

After the usual formalities, the conversation went like this:

> PROCTOR: Would you be so good as to introduce me to this young lady?
>
> OXBRITE (*Thinking fast*): Of course, sir. This is my sister.
>
> PROCTOR (*Taking him aside*): Are you aware that this is the most notorious whore in Oxford?
>
> OXBRITE (*Thinking faster*): Yes, sir. Mother and I are terribly worried about her.

To show just how serious the situation has been, some comparative figures will be helpful. These are for Oxford, but the point is made for both universities:

YEAR	MALE UNDERGRADUATES	FEMALE UNDERGRADUATES
1922	4,803	949
1932	5,675	984
1942	5,977	1,049
1952	8,144	1,244
1962	7,688	1,287

It gets better over the last few years, with the advent of co-residence at colleges hitherto male. In 1968 there were 9,208 male Oxbrites at Cambridge, and only 1,208 female, whereas the figures for 1982/3 were 5,698:3,296 (Oxford), and 6,498:3,106 (Cambridge); projected 1984 Oxford admissions were 4,453:3110 (much healthier) at the time of writing.

Clare, King's and Churchill opened their doors to women in 1972, and Hertford, Jesus, Exeter, Brasenose and Wadham were the first to follow suit at Oxford in 1974. There were still difficulties. At Hertford, men were forbidden to enter women's rooms; but no one had forbidden the women undergraduates to push their furniture into the corridors for social occasions. Oxbrites met a new challenge with traditional ingenuity.

The co-residential college has been a qualified success. Many younger Oxbrites join forces with older ones against the idea for different reasons. Older Oxbrites dislike it because they cannot bear the thought of their old college playing host to the opposite sex. Younger ones have seen how like an unpleasant little village or similar closed society co-residence can make a college. 'I've just broken up with a guy on my staircase – he dumped me – and now I think how great it must be to be in a women's college. I wouldn't have to see him at breakfast every day with his new girl', wailed one, and it is interesting to see also how she casts herself in the subordinate role – a tendency which is still common, even though the numbers are evening up; and a tendency which is rather strengthened than weakened by co-residency. Lots of washing and ironing is done for the lads. Co-residence is further insidious in that colleges no longer cross-fertilize. A more equal number of one-sex colleges would have been a better idea. Perhaps those colleges founded by women should have been the first to change the sex of their intake – though one can imagine the effect on old male scouts, gyps and dons.

Attitudes to all this have been fun. The first female intake to Clare and King's was declared to be lesbian, *en bloc*. The first male intake to LMH was declared to be a bunch of poufs. Now that the enthusiasm has died down, and women have been discovered *not* to have a particularly civilizing effect on college hearties, as was fondly hoped, we can discuss some of the sex problems which Oxbrites delight in talking about, swapping yarns of the battlefield as veterans do who are the survivors of some especially ghastly campaign.

Things were so desperate in the fifties that one Oxbrite of that vintage remembers that you couldn't even afford to be selective: 'After one bottle of 3s. 9d. plonk any woman was pretty.' His sentiments are echoed by an Oxbrite who in 1968 gave vent to, 'Christ, I'm so randy I could tackle a tree in a kilt', and by the one who, ditching her first boyfriend, remarked, 'One down, nine to go.' Even in those rigid and discriminatory days, strong men were driven to homosexuality and drink by the lack of women, or a fear of them born of their scarcity. On the other hand, grammar school plain Janes who'd never had a man look at them suddenly found themselves besieged, and sometimes reacted like a starving man might when unexpectedly confronted with a feast. For a society of intellectual people, those who called the shots at Oxbridge were behaving with a remarkable lack of intelligence (they would call it a lack of worldliness). The situation was unhappy. Worse, for colonials unused to the more refined ways of the world, the offer of a glass of sherry, analogous to the hand of friendship in Oxbridge circles, was regarded as the sure sign of a homosexual advance.

In the fifties, a simple set of unofficial rules about women's behaviour was drawn up. If you got a woman back to your rooms you were, in theory, in like Flynn, *provided that she took her shoes off.* If you were seducing a woman, you should do so to the accompaniment of Frank Sinatra's 'Songs for Swinging Lovers', side one. If you hadn't made it by 'It Happened in Monterey', you wouldn't. Some fifties Oxbrites still cannot bear to listen to this record.

It is symptomatic of the nature of the obsession that these theories grew up among undergraduates who were not just the run-of-the-mill, wet-behind-the-ears Oxbrites of preceding and succeeding years, but who included men who had killed for their country in a six-year war, who had travelled the world and commanded soldiers.

Prostitutes had priced themselves above the undergraduate pocket by the end of the fifties, and in any case as

besieged

they are considered to be the last resort of the truly desperate, they have for many years been considered *out*, especially as the prostitutes of Northern Europe in general
carry with them an appalling, Victorian-front-parlour

morality which is as dispiriting as the smell of dust in an unused room. Oxford undergraduates of the early-to-mid sixties therefore remember with enthusiastic affection a one-woman self-appointed social service known as 'Black Jenny'.

Described as 'pox'd like the Devil' by the earthier kind of Oxbrite, my researches have led me to the conclusion that this was probably untrue, but that she certainly had a generous, gregarious and even gorgeous nature: she led every male (and the occasional female) Oxbrite who wished it painlessly through his First Time. She was not 'black' in the sense of 'negro', but she had long straight black hair and wore black trouser suits. She wore white lipstick, said 'Hey, man' a good deal, and worked as a model at the Ruskin. She was a painter herself ('of the Nightmare School'), and is described by one defloweree as being 'at the spearhead of the hippy culture ... and she seemed, you know, so old, and so wise. I expect she must have been about 26.' Her father was supposed by popular tradition to be an unfrocked Gay vicar. The most fondly remembered story about her is that she once went to a Commem. Ball wearing nothing but a sheet. Of course someone immediately accidentally-on-purpose sprayed a bottle of champagne over her so that the sheet clung lovingly to every contour of her body. I have seen several pairs of eyes go misty at this memory.

Black Jenny, with a fine sense of appropriateness, lived in Paradise Square. She no longer lives in Oxford, and the author would die rather than reveal her current whereabouts.

Oxford men of the time who were lucky enough to need them bought their condoms from a surgical store in New Inn Hall Street – from a small, elderly and disapproving man whose barbed comments seemed more the result of envy than disapproval. The barber in All Saints' Passage was the source of Durex for most Cambridge undergraduates. He was a much more endearing character. One Oxbrite had four haircuts in nine days, in his attempt to pluck up the courage to buy a 'packet of three'. At the end of the fourth haircut the barber asked his habitual, 'And will there be anything else, sir?', and got the usual flustered silence. Gazing at the shorn and blushing head in front of him, he added admonishingly, 'I hope we won't be losing the girls with the curls, sir.'

Getting to meet the opposite sex wasn't easy unless you were invited to parties, and then there was always the danger (it still exists) of getting there and seeing no one but established couples, and other people of your own sex. At Oxford, various dances would occasionally be organized by the town (see above), and by the Union (if you were after a woman undergraduate, these were the ones to go to), but there was never any guarantee of success. Conquests were something to be shown off. A bribable scout or gyp was an advantage, as we have seen, and could lead in especially liberal circumstances not only to an uninterrupted 'morning after', but even two cups of tea! Otherwise an Oxford conquest would be treated to breakfast at the Randolph or the Mitre – preferably at the most visible table possible. Twenty years ago, Corpus (Oxford) men even had the architecture against them: it has always been a difficult college to climb into, but never more so than for a girl dressed in the fashions of the mid-sixties.

If social life through the media of invitations, dances and society notices on the Screens (see Glossary) fail to turn anything up for you, you could be in for a hard graft, spending a good deal of money and time tracking down a woman, or (if you are a woman) avoiding unwanted attentions, or getting involved too soon with too many, or just with the wrong one. Lots of women undergraduates have carved themselves out terrible reputations simply by being too polite or too nervous to say 'no'.

Most Oxbrites will have a Thin Time during their first

year on the sex front, so you might as well steel yourself for it. Do not despair, though. Life can smile too, as the following story (a very useful one for retelling as your own) illustrates:

An Oxford undergraduate had for some time been singularly unlucky with women, and was thus condemned by his peers to what was graphically called the Outer Gobbley Circle. But one summer evening at the end of his first year he found himself in the company of an LMH girl at a party at the Cherwell Boat House. He was flushed with success at a recent prank: changing round all the heraldic shields on all the college boathouses on the Isis; and the LMH girl seemed rather to admire him for this. Encouraged by her, he managed to steal a punt, and in it the two of them drifted downstream towards her college (he couldn't get a punt pole as they were all locked up). It was a balmy night, conducive to a little physical exploration, and that seemed like a good idea to both of them. His excitement (the author regrets that he is only able to tell this story from the point of view of the storyteller) mounted as he found himself allowed to cross further and further frontiers. Finally, as the punt came to rest against the grassy bank of the river, his fingers were allowed to stray into what John Donne calls 'India'. Things went no further, but he had taken a vital step along the road of sexual initiation, and, what was more, he could now hold his head up as a Member of the *Inner* Gobbley Circle.

A not dissimilar story illustrates how suddenly and unexpectedly sex can steal up on the Oxbrite. One such remembers how at a party he met a Venezuelan girl. He was struck by the fact that she was wearing an ankle-length fur coat, but he soon forgot about details because their eyes met across the crowded room, and it was lust at first sight. He took her back to his rooms immediately, and she took off her coat: she had nothing on underneath. They made love passionately and without any preamble on a Union Jack he used as a bedspread, *all night*. In the morning she left and he only ever saw her once more, at another party, where no further vital spark was struck. She remains one of the most important people in his life, although he never knew her name.

Sexual intensity can lead to awkward situations too, though. An Oxbrite once bedded down (drunk) on a mattress on the floor with a male friend, who was already asleep (drunk) in his rooms. The girlfriend of the moment let herself in the following morning, saw them, immediately assumed that they were Gay, and shrieked histrionically. The Oxbrite says he still has nightmares about being awakened by that shriek!

But this is Oxford, and we know the male undergraduates here do not like their female counterparts. One female Oxbrite complained to me, 'We were regarded as totally unsuitable, by virtue of our intellect, which was thought dangerous; even if we were socially OK, it was felt that we wouldn't make good wives and mothers, as we would be too bright to know our place.'

Many Oxbrites *do* know their place, however, or at any rate think they do. At the end of the final year at Oxbridge, there is always a rash of marriages, as people decide that they will be unable to face the World Outside without each other (i.e. without kindred spirits). Some of these marriages actually work, but they are all a symptom of the *Après Nous le Déluge* delusion that affects a lot of Oxbrites on the verge of departure. One whole bunch of Footlights people at the end of the sixties even wrote a maudlin song about themselves, called 'The Party's Moving On'. The obverse, however, happens too, and I have uncovered plenty of evidence to suggest that as many relationships end on the rocks as do in marriage during the final hectic weeks before The End. After all, all that concentrated work and concentrated pleasure, all at once, and then over forever, creates the kind of tension from which many

Oxbrites never recover. The break-ups occur because, some say, going through that unique and bittersweet valedictory experience together in a sense otherwise condemns and commits you to a lifetime together. Others disagree, pointing out that the majority of relationships bonded during the three years at Oxbridge perish anyway within nine months of the weather of the World Outside.

Nearly all Oxbrites are virgins when they arrive. This is because they come from nice backgrounds and/or single-sex schools. The unwonted freedom they suddenly get at Oxbridge makes them feel adult, and they seek the imprimatur of Nature on adulthood – the Losing of the Virginity. This immediately assumes an importance and a significance out of all proportion to the act.

A Cambridge undergraduate slept quite innocently on various men friends' sofas until she discovered that she had acquired a deep-scarlet reputation as a tease and that bets were running between *six* colleges on who would take her virginity first. She was even regarded as a kind of Elinor Glyn by one particular Oxbrite, who came up to her one day bleating, 'Can you educate me?', with an appropriate leer. When she finally did surrender her virtue, it was to a man at Catz. That he was not what she took him for she quickly discovered, for a few weeks later they were surprised in his rooms by the arrival of the bedder. He popped our heroine naked into his wardrobe, and threw her clothes in after her. The bedder entered, and 'Andrea', naked in the dark, heard her boyfriend wilt before the woman's suspicion; and she was aghast when she heard him say to her, 'Ehrm – I'm just going off to a lecture now. Do clean the room', and left. 'Andrea' stayed in the wardrobe, hardly daring to breathe, until after what seemed an eternity of cleaning the bedder opened the wardrobe. Both 'Andrea' and her boyfriend were reported.

She later got rid of this awful first lover in a novel way,

which is worth remembering. She was giving him a lift on the pillion of her motorbike from Market Hill to Catz. On the way she was invited to race by another Oxbrite on a more powerful machine. Her boyfriend made one wimpish remark too many and she kicked down the gear from third to second, instead of up to fourth. This had the effect of standing the bike up, and 'loverboy fell off. He still has the scars, I'm happy to say'.

An abundance of men can lead women to excess, and then they can acquire bad reputations. An Oxbrite to whom this happened found herself seduced by an American Ivy League type whom we will call 'Jonty'. He then ditched her – which left her thirsting for revenge. She gathered friends around her and decided to attack him through his weakest point – his snobbery.

Jonty was persuaded to give a cocktail party for the daughter of Haile Selassie. He swallowed this because the person who asked the favour was the son of the Ethiopian Ambassador. The 'princess' duly arrived with a small entourage and two black 'bodyguards' (all Oxbrites whom Jonty had never seen before). The 'princess' was of course our heroine, blacked up and wearing a braided wig. She got away with it partly because the disguise was skilful, and partly because one of her friends had, in 'trying on' the shortsighted American's new spectacles, managed to cover the lenses with grease from peanutty fingers, which Jonty was unable to remove adequately.

From the cocktail party, they all went on to Don Pasquale's – one of the most expensive restaurants in town – and at dinner the 'princess' started to touch Jonty up under the table in a quite outrageous way. He was torn between embarrassment and complacency, and by the end of the evening had committed himself to a weekend in Paris with the lady, followed by a winter's skiing 'in the Ethiopian highlands'.

The following day our heroine took Jonty round a huge

bouquet, and told him the truth. He took it very badly.

One Oxbrite, entering Cambridge from a liberal, co-educational public school (Bedales), had as his first depressing thought, 'Here I am in a city without women!' In the same term that saw an inflatable doll hoisted to the top of King's porters' lodge, he lost the girlfriend he had brought with him from school. 'Georgiana' was not in his rooms as she had promised to be when he returned one evening from performing in a play. Acting on a horrible premonition, he went round to his best friend's rooms and quickly established, by hammering on the door and yelling, that 'Georgiana' and he were together in there, and that they weren't making cupcakes. Unable to gain access, our hero stormed through the adjoining room, where a couple of harmless mathematicians were playing chess and drinking Newcastle Brown, and climbed out of the window onto the ledge – it was three floors up. He edged along to his friend's window and burst in at it, pulling the bedclothes from the intimidated lovers, who said, 'You bastard!' (she); and 'Oh, my God!' (he), as our hero dragged her up out of the bed. Later, the best friend was Contrite, and was Forgiven – on the understanding that *he never did it again*; but he did, of course, and finally took 'Georgiana' off our hero's hands – he was half saddened and half relieved.

Another aspect of sex in the seventies at Cambridge was the Mazola party. The dynamic of such events was simple. People would put an oil-cloth on the floor of a room, strip off, and pour Mazola oil over each other. Alternatively, people would 'streak' across college courts between the stripping off and the pouring on of the Mazola. But this engaging craze was unfortunately shortlived, owing to the difficulty of clearing up afterwards, and the rising cost of Mazola.

Gay Oxbrites now have their own societies and organizations, and with them their own social scene. There is no social barrier of Town and Gown, so they are particularly fortunate. Of course there always *was* a social scene for Gays, the myth that there wasn't being perpetrated by the more organization-minded lesbians and the more wimpish homosexual men. One anecdote will suffice. A future novelist and a future eminent cleric were lunching together at the Varsity restaurant one day when the attention of the cleric was attracted to the tightness of their waiter's trousers. 'I think,' he said, 'that I have never seen anyone wearing such tight trousers.' 'Then,' said the novelist, 'let us leave him an extraordinarily large tip, and our telephone numbers.'

The unfortunate side-effect of public acceptance is that Gays now have to suffer, like everyone else, the tension of having their affairs subjected to the public scrutiny and gossip in which Oxbridge delights.

The fledgling Oxbrite should simply cling to his/her copy of *The Little Blue Book* (which was not available to older Oxbrites), and, taking its contents with a handful of salt, along with any other advice, travel hopefully. Where sex is concerned it is nearly always better to do that than to arrive in any case, and in later life many Oxbrites simply revert to their two standard vices, drinking too much and talking too much. If you meet an older male Oxbrite who wants to reminisce about sex, and you want to avoid the subject, just tell him you didn't get any because you had to share rooms. He will understand perfectly, and quite possibly turn the conversation to Sport.

〖13〗

Sport

SPORT IS A much easier subject to deal with because you know where you are with it. You do a specific job, either on your own or in a team, but in any case with someone to tell you how to do it, and to tick you off if you do it wrongly or unfairly, and in the end you have either won or lost. There are no distressing blurry edges with sport, and it has flourished obstinately, despite a Vice-Chancellor's decree of 1595 'that the hurtfull and unscolerlike exercise of Football and meetings tending to that end, do from henceforth utterly cease'.

There are, however, still things for the budding Oxbrite to learn. The first concerns the vexed question of Blues and Half Blues. What are they, and how do you get them?

Not all sports merit a Full Blue; some only rate a Half Blue, and some don't get anything at all. Blues are awarded solely by the captain of the sport, and normally only to those who represent the university against *the other place*.[1] However, Athletics presents an immediate problem, because only the first string usually gets a Blue – the second string only gets one too if they are really terrific; and in swimming you only get a Full Blue if you can achieve a standard set time. Older Oxbrites take note that swimming has only merited a Full Blue since the mid-sixties.

There is a Blues Committee of course, which is made up of a bunch of people who are very good at sport – usually Full Blue captains and presidents of the various dominant

[1] See Glossary.

sports – and they determine the status of individual sports. All applications for Blue status must be put before a committee meeting.

In the bad old days, women could only ever merit Half Blues for playing Oxford (or Cambridge); they could only get a Full Blue by participating in the British Universities' Sports Federation competition.

All sportsmen tell you that it's great fun 'at third team level', but the fact remains that they take it all with grim seriousness; and that all male sportsmen are still deeply prejudiced against women. However, although the great days of Oxbridge sport are long gone (they had their heyday at the turn of the century, when getting a Blue *did* mean more than getting a First, and when colleges really *did* take undergraduates on board for their sporting ability alone), sport is no longer considered quite as *out* as it was ten or fifteen years ago. That this is so is due to two factors:

(a) the keep-fit craze (and Raquel Welch in particular)
(b) the increasing *presence* of women (even though they don't necessarily compete against men, they are at least around).

The Oxbrite wishing to claim a Blue or a Half Blue should be careful to choose the right sport for it. No use saying you've got a Blue in fencing – you'll be found out.

Here is a helpful checklist:

BLUES	HALF BLUES
Association football	Archery
Athletics	Ballroom dancing
Basketball	Canoeing
Boats (Rowing)	Croquet
Boxing	Cycling
Cricket	Eton Fives
Cross Country	Fencing
Golf	Gymnastics

BLUES	HALF BLUES
Hockey	Ice hockey
Lawn tennis	Judo
Netball	Karate
Rugby *Union*	Lacrosse
Squash	Modern Pentathlon
Swimming	Orienteering
Yachting	Pistols
	Rackets
	Real tennis
	Riding
	Rifles
	Rugby Fives
	Rugby *League*
	Skiing
	Sul Ki Do
	Table tennis
	Volleyball
	Water polo

Source: Oxford, 1984
Note: Older Oxbrites should not attempt to claim Karate
or Sul Ki Do.

Be careful if you are awarding yourself a Blue or a Half
Blue with the intention of using it in genuine Oxbridge
sporting circles. Sporting Oxbrites take it all very
seriously and continue to do so throughout life (unless the
drink gets them). Sport provides such a simple and
effective answer to, and escape from, most of life's
problems, that, rather like religion, once discovered it
cannot easily be given up. The next question to be settled
is what sports are currently *in* and *out*, and for once this is
not too difficult to answer. Although the rise of the lower
class at Oxbridge has meant a certain development of
popularity for Association Football, and although cricket

has its following (Annual Varsity match at Lord's), there really are only two sports that count at Oxbridge:

(a) Rugby Union
(b) Rowing.

The long haul towards representing your university in the Varsity Match demands blind dedication, and as far as rugby[1] is concerned the Oxbrite[2] will find himself playing league matches in the Michaelmas term and 'Cuppers'[3] – inter-college knockout competitions – in the Lent term. The apogee of a male career is to play in the Varsity Match at Twickenham at the end of the Michaelmas term. Even non-Oxbrites flock to this, and more alcohol is consumed than ever. À propos alcohol, it should be noted that ruggerbuggers are essentially beer-drinkers. At Twickenham in 1982 the tradition of an hour's hard boozing at the ground's bars following the match was interrupted when the police (a very non-Oxbridge organization, despite the colour of its uniform) had them closed. This measure was in response to complaints from local residents of rowdiness following the 1981 match. In 1983, the police once again tried to have all the bars remain closed, except for the luxurious Rose Room in the South Stand. This would have effectively spelt disaster for carousing Oxbridge ruggerbuggers, because the Rose Room is expensive, and emphatically not the place for a drunken orgy. Luckily for them the chairman of the Richmond licensing justices ruled that the police proposal would discriminate against 'the *hoi polloi*', thus rather cleverly turning the tables on the police and restoring a noble tradition in Oxbridge rugby circles.

Good ruggerbugger colleges are St Edmund Hall at Oxford and Fitzwilliam at Cambridge.

[1] And other, less significant, team winter sports.
[2] No women's rugby team has yet been formed.
[3] At Cambridge; not to be confused with Oxford 'Cuppers'.

Bumps

The king of sports at Oxbridge is rowing. Each college has at least one boat, and most have several, and they compete against each other, within their own universities, on two major occasions per year. Trials for would-be rowers are held in the Michaelmas term.

Races at Oxbridge are called Bumps. Because of the narrowness of the rivers available, the boats cannot race abreast; they are accordingly divided into Divisions. The aim of every crew is to become Head of the River, which is the name given to the crew at the top of the first division. However, since a crew will probably only advance one place in any one race, it is much more realistic to reduce your ambition to getting one 'bump' on each of the four racing days of each meeting. This is how it works: a 'bump' occurs when a pursuing boat either hits the one ahead, or forces the alarmed cox sitting at the end of it to concede. He is more than likely to do this: in the first series of Lent races at Cambridge in 1888, E. S. Campbell was rowing at 4 in the Clare boat. Clare had just drawn into the bank at First Post Corner after making its third bump, when a Trinity Hall boat, trying to wash off a pursuing Emmanuel crew, collided with Clare, and Campbell was pierced through the heart by its bows. There is something persuasive about the sharp end of an Eights boat approaching your kidneys with speed. The pursuing cox will call for a 'stroke ten' – ten strokes of extra effort to effect the bump.

Once a bump has been achieved, both boats retire from the race for that day, the winner taking the loser's position on the following day. At Cambridge a twig is placed in the stern of the victors' boat behind the cox to show supporters on the shore who have missed seeing the bump that it has been achieved. A lot of bumps take place during the early stages of the race, so canny Oxbrites who are keen spectators and not just there for the Pimm's will watch from as close to the starting lines as possible, where the crews are grouped in order of their place in the division, one and a half boat-lengths apart. If a boat neither bumps nor is bumped, the crew have to 'row over' the whole length of the course. At Oxford the Oriel crew, who have been Head of the River for several years past, have to do this every day of Eights Week. Apparently they do not mind.

Consolation for losers is non-existent, but in a crew managing to bump its way up four places on four consecutive days, each oarsman 'wins his blade'. The oar he has pulled, duly autographed by all his fellow crew members, is his to keep as a souvenir for ever, which need not be a problem so long as he always lives somewhere where at least one room is over ten feet in length. At the end of the race meeting, coxes get thrown into the river, and the Head of the River burns an old boat in celebration. They may go further. Some years ago, when Keble was Head, the triumphant boaties not only burnt their boat, but all the quad staircase doors too. They then played frisbee with the college soup plates. Post-rowing junketing is a good thing to avoid if you are of an aesthetic or nervous disposition. Many arty Oxbrites will know nothing at all of boat racing (except of course for the Boat Race), but in the World Outside the most unlikely male Oxbrite will thrill again in memory to the atmosphere by the river bank, as, girl on arm, blazer on back, boater (see Glossary) – with the college colours on its band – on head, Pimm's in hand, and strawberries and cream in mouth, he hears the cheering, and the piercing note of the horns telling the crews that victory approaches.

Would-be Oxbrites, having digested all the infor- tion given above, should now address themselves to some simple facts.

At Oxford, the Hilary term races are called Torpids (or Toggers – see Glossary), and are rowed in February. At Cambridge, the Lent races are called 'Lents'. The fifth week of Trinity term is Eights Week at Oxford (not to be confused with the eighth week, which is, of course, the eighth week; 'Eights' refers to the crews – eight oarsmen and a cox – of the Eights boats; there are, of course, *other* boats, but as these are of less distinction I shall not bother you with them here). In the Easter term at Cambridge, the 'Mays' are rowed.

The *course* at Oxford runs from just below Donnington Bridge to just below Folly Bridge on the Isis, with the boathouses ranged along the south-western side of the triangular island below Christ Church Meadow. The Cambridge course is between Baitsbite Lock and Midsummer Common, on the Cam. Until 1892, the 'Mays' concluded with a Boat Procession past King's lawn. The boats were decked with flowers, and the Head of the River toasted in wine. Then everyone toasted everyone else, and threw flowers at each other. The author finds it difficult to imagine what modern Oxbridge boaties would make of such a custom, but feels that he should point out that, for the first few years of the Boat Race, before they took to wearing light blue in 1836, Cambridge men distinguished themselves from Oxford by wearing pink sashes.

At Oxford, only St Catherine's still supports a college barge, alas. Best views are from the boathouse roofs, and their bars are open all day in Eights Week.

The Boat Race is the one thing *everybody* knows about Oxbridge. It is rowed on the Thames between Putney and Mortlake, a four-mile distance, in early Spring. Once an event to turn London on its head, it still attracts vast crowds, and the *hoi polloi* have even invented loyal songs about it, which is a little presumptuous of them, but well-meaning, no doubt. The race lasts about twenty minutes, and is divided into four recognizable sections, identified by landmarks: Harrod's Wall, one mile out, takes about four minutes to reach. Then come Chiswick Steps, Barnes Bridge and Mortlake Brewery. The race is judged by an umpire, and at the beginning the crew winning the toss can opt for the 'Surrey' (south bank), or 'Middlesex' (north bank) station. Surrey is better because it takes advantage of the river's bend, but if the boat on the Middlesex station is winning it may cross over to the Surrey side and 'take the other boat's water'. Each boat has an Eights crew, and the race remains the preserve of men; although there have been female coxes, no Ladies'

Boat Race has yet been set up. First man is called 'stroke'. Rowlocks are called 'riggers'. The biggest men are placed in the middle of the boat, and they really are big, weighing $14\frac{1}{2}$–$15\frac{1}{2}$ stone. Often they come from America. The boats are called the Blue Boats.

There are in fact two races, though television watchers only see the main one, which is preceded by one between the reserve teams. The reserve teams' boats are called *Isis* (Oxford) and *Goldie* (Cambridge). Latterly, the Boat Race has been taken over by commercial sponsorship and now rejoices under such titles as 'The Ladbroke University Boat Race' – to the disgust of most Oxbrites, whether or not they are interested in the race itself.

Until recently, Cambridge habitually won the Boat Race, but in recent years they have been regularly trounced by Oxford. The number of wins at the time of writing, however, is 68 to Cambridge and 62 to Oxford, so that both sides still have everything to play for. However, in 1985 Oxford won for the tenth successive year. Good rowing colleges are Oriel at Oxford, and St John's and Trinity at Cambridge.

For non-athletic swimmers (a pastime more than a sport) Oxford provides Parsons' Pleasure for male nude bathing. On the Cherwell just above Music Meadow, women must disempunt before reaching it and pass behind a strategically-placed privet hedge before regaining their craft. Dames' Delight, nearby, is for female nude bathing. One wonders why the names are not exchanged – it would surely be more logical? At Cambridge, Byron's Pool has tenuous connections with that aquatic Lord, and the Bathing Shed was for many years a notable haunt of the Gay community.

There is a third sport which must be mentioned to complete even the briefest introduction to the social life of the Oxbrite. No Blues, or even Half Blues, are available from it, and yet participation in it is more or less a *sine qua non* for all Oxbrites, whether they are by inclination sporting or not. It is punting.

The punt is a long, flat, shallow boat with a platform deck at one end (to distinguish that end from the other), propelled by a long pole with an open double-hook at one end. It can take up to half a dozen people (more if tourists are involved), but the ideal occupancy is two. Of these two, one punts, and one lies back on the cushions (preferably on the forward seat, so that she faces the punter), dressed prettily. Her task is to keep the wine cool, and to look admiringly at the punter. The action of the punter depends on his ability to punt, but if he is a true professional and can keep the water on the punt pole from running down his sleeves, he will also be able to dress prettily. Punting is easier than it looks, but it requires practice to:

(a) keep the punt on course, and
(b) avoid falling in.

Keeping the punt on course involves dropping the pole straight down by the side of the punt and parallel to it before pushing downwards and backwards to propel it forwards. To steer left or right, manoeuvre the slack pole trailing behind the moving punt against your thigh to the left (behind you) or right. Feet should at all times be static, and kept in contact with the punt. Hands should grasp the pole firmly at all times unless it sticks in the mud at the bottom of the river, when it should be let go of. In such a case you will lose the pole if you let go, but you will fall in if you don't. To retrieve the pole you may paddle the punt back to where it has stuck, but apart from such an extreme case the paddle provided with the punt should *never* be used.[1] In fact, the paddle should never be used,

[1] Except in the case of dongola racing – see below. Oxford Oxbrites may use a paddle on deeper parts of the Cherwell, too.

full stop, since the pole should never be lost. The pole is normally let fall into the river on the right-hand side of the punt, and truly expert punters will be able to produce a fair turn of speed, in time, by developing the technique of twirling the pole out of the water and punting end over end. The author has even seen this developed (once) to the point of being achieved *one-handed* (by, let it be said *sotto voce*, a Townie); but such artistry should only be attempted by the singularly adept.

The main purpose of punting is, however, relaxation. At Cambridge you punt between Jesus Lock and Mill Pit along the Backs of the colleges (Lower Cam). This is easy punting for most of its length because the river is shallow and has a gravel bottom, although you need to get speed up towards Queens' Mathematical Bridge because there it is deeper and muddier. Alternatively you can take a punt along the quieter and more rural Upper Cam (sometimes still called the Granta) towards Grantchester – which is relatively tourist-free, but deeper and muddier all the way. There used to be a slipway by the Mill Pit weir up or down which punts could be slid, so that the whole length of the Cam from Grantchester to Jesus Lock could be navigated, but this appears to have gone. Punts can be hired for the Granta at Scudamore's, Granta Place; and for the backs at Scudamore's, Mill Lane; the Anchor, Silver Street; Scudamore's, Magdalene Bridge; and Tyrell's, Magdalene Bridge. Most Backs colleges also have their own punts, painted (at least the tops of their poles) in college colours. For the tourist, or fledgling Oxbrite scared of responsibility, a new facility has grown up in recent years: at Silver Street Bridge Chauffeurpunts will hire you a punt with a driver for £2.50 per person for a forty-minute tour of the Backs; and Picnic Punts for a little more will do the same with a hamper thrown in (as it were). Dearer than do-it-yourself, these schemes must be turning over more than pennies for the enterprising Oxbrites who have initiated them as a way of earning money in the Long Vacs.

Although Cambridge is *the* place for punting, it must be acknowledged that Oxford does it too – though without the picturesque advantage of the Backs. Although Oxford has two rivers, the Isis[1] is really too deep for such a gentle sport (although it can be attempted if you get a special licence), and is generally left to the more manly (or womanly) rowers. It is the Cherwell that punters usually turn to, dawdling along to such places as the Cherwell Boat House and the Vicky Arms, and in general doing all the things that Cambridge Oxbrites do in punts, with two important distinctions:

(a) they use metal punt poles
(b) they punt from the wrong end.

These departures require explanation. No self-respecting punt-person would ever use anything but a wooden pole, and yet at Oxford they do! There seems to be no reason or excuse for this extraordinary vulgarity. Nor does there seem to be any logic behind the perversity with which they punt from the wrong end. All *proper* punts are built with a platform deck at at least one end (and some Oxford punts don't even have this!); its purpose is clear: to be stood upon when one is punting. At Oxford they eschew this reasonable facility and stand at the other, sloping end – a course of action which incidentally makes punting harder to do. However, Cambridge Oxbrites punting at Oxford should take note of the maxim, 'When in Rome . . .', rather than subject themselves to the jeers of the grockle-like Oxford Oxbrites, who will otherwise think they are – at worst – tourists.

Oxford punts are available from the Cherwell Boat

---

[1] It's the Thames, actually, but Oxonians call it the Isis from its Latin name – *Thamesis*. Nothing to do with the Egyptian goddess.

House, Bardwell Road; Howard's, Magdalen Bridge; Hubbucks and Riverside Boating, Folly Bridge.

At both Oxford and Cambridge *real* grockles can hire canoes and even (at Oxford) motor boats. Oxbrites would die rather than do this, although gondolas (*much* more difficult than punts) have been seen driven by Oxbrites on the Cam.

Attached to punting are two *nebensächliche* sports, each exclusive to its respective university.

At Oxford on 20 June 1984 was revived – much to the author's and ancient Oxbrites' delight – the noble sport of dongola racing, in abeyance since 1922, when it was interdicted by a reactionary Vice-Chancellor. The sport, revived to mark the centenary of Lord Wolseley's Nile expedition to relieve General Gordon at Khartoum (described by *The Times* of 1884 as 'the longest Boat Race in history'), covers a 300-yard course on the Isis, from the Boat Houses to Folly Bridge. The word 'dongola' derives from the town of Dongola on the Nile, the objective of Wolseley's 370-mile journey (he offered a prize of £100 to the first boat to reach it), and is not an anagram of 'gondola'. The race made its début at Maidenhead Regatta in 1886. The craft used are punts, the method of propulsion paddles and the crews are made up of four men and two women. Crews are essentially untrained, but the race is a test of watermanship, because fast-moving punts set up a wide bow wave, and they lack both rudders and keel.

At Cambridge, the number of bridges over the river along the Backs affords the opportunity of another sport: punt pole seizing. Not all the bridges are good for this, some being too high, but Magdalene, Trinity and (especially) Clare provide excellent points of vantage. The seizer waits until the unwary punter below has his pole lifted at maximum height, vertically clear of the river, and then plucks it from him, leaving him to drift angrily and helplessly away. A delightful and unfortunately only once-achieved variant of this concerned two Clare undergraduates. Clare Bridge is decorated with an array of large stone balls. The Oxbrites made a polystyrene replica of one, and, positioning it on the parapet, waited for suitable victims. They found the ideal subjects: a punt-load of Nikon-clicking Japanese tourists, complete with grey raglan raincoats and tartan bobble hats. With acting worthy of an Olivier, they pushed and grunted with the effort of dislodging their 'ball', to the panic of the Japanese, who threw themselves into the Cam, Nikons and all. The 'ball', of course, floated gently down to rest harmlessly on the vacated punt. Alas, the perpetrators were rusticated for their deed. It is the view of the author that they should have been rewarded – for originality, if not for xenophobia.

One final word on punting comes as a caveat to passengers from Dorothy L. Sayers (a Somerville Oxbrite): 'I admit it is more fun to punt than to be punted, and that the desire to have all the fun is nine-tenths of the law of chivalry.'

【14】

Vacations

VACATIONS ARE generally known as 'vacs', and they are the same as holidays. Except that they aren't. The Oxbrite is quickly disabused of the illusion that weeks and even months of generous holiday punctuate his academic career. The shorter vacs, about five weeks at Christmas and Easter, just about give you time to draw breath, resent being at home and earn a few bob to supplement the next term's grant, or help pay off debts incurred during the last one. The Long Vac is the challenge. Most Oxbrites get two during their academic career, from June until October. These four months theoretically give you time to travel to far-flung places, or to carve at least a foothold in a career in preparation for the World Outside. In fact, half the time is usually spent working to get some grant supplement (again), and the other half catching up on the *vita academica*. Keen undergraduates will go up for the Long Vac Term, a sort of midsummer work-in; some subjects require it, and if you're changing subjects you'll almost certainly have to do it. Older Oxbrites remember the Hippy Trail, and Discovering America, but many just frittered the time away. It is nothing to be ashamed of, but it is a constant source of regret later, for Life never gives most people so much free time again. The same, in fact, could be said of Oxbridge in general: it is a world between two cages; that of school and parental authority, and that of Work, and family responsibility of your own. Having once tasted the freedom of letting their minds wander at liberty on a small but effective 'private income', many Oxbrites never come to terms with the latter cage; and many that do succumb to it hark back to their three years in Academe as some old soldiers do to the Second World War: to the one time in their lives when they had adventure, and the freedom to be themselves.

Always provided, of course, that looking for digs and sitting exams didn't give them nightmares.

⟦15⟧

Pranks, Protests and Sidelines

No OxBRITES worth their salt will be without a number of anecdotes about what they did when they were 'up'. Would-be Oxbrites should never be daunted by what they hear; they should bear in mind Falstaff's opinion of Robert Shallow: 'Lord, Lord, how subject we old men are to this vice of lying!' As ammunition, I offer a small selection of pranks and sidelines suitable for insertion into any conversation that turns to reminiscence. Most of them are true.

Enthusiasm for Oxford was upheld by Samuel Johnson: 'He delighted in his own partiality for Oxford, and one day, at my house, entertained five members of the other university with various instances of the superiority of Oxford . . . At last I said to him, "Why there happens to be no less than five Cambridge men in the room now." "I did not (said he) think of that till you told me; but the wolf don't count the sheep." ' (Hester Lynch Piozzi, *Anecdotes of the Late Samuel Johnson,* 1786.) The same vulgar enthusiasm for the place (and so typical of it) spread abroad. One verse of P. de Mascarène's 'Ode à Oxford' (1845) says it all:

'Comment parler d'Oxford, sans dire quelque chose
'De ses bons habitants? Si j'écrivais en prose,
'Au lieu d'en nommer trois: Wootten, Wingfield, Thomson,
'J'en pourrais citer cent avec même raison.'

Thirty years after that ornament was written, Oscar Wilde went up to Magdalen. He quickly attracted attention as an aesthete, and some college boaties made the mistake of thinking that he was also a wimp. Four of them got tight, and burst into his rooms, intending (an example of Oxbridge thinking at its subtlest) to smash his furniture and drink his booze. Unfortunately for them Wilde was as strong as he was big. He threw three of them out, and carried the ringleader bodily to *his* rooms, where he smashed *his* furniture, and invited the turncoat mob who'd come out to watch the fun to drink *his* booze. They did this all the more eagerly because the ringleader was renowned for stinginess. Wilde was never bothered again.

Ancient Oxbrites will remember the twenties when women were really good and unemancipated. Among the rules they had to cope with were: 'Mixed parties may not be held in cafés before 2 p.m. or after 5.30 p.m. Between these hours they are permitted, provided that permission has been granted beforehand, and that there are at least two women in the party.' Several girls were sent down for disguising themselves as men and thus getting into male Halls – though their male accomplices were let off with warnings. The would-be Oxbrite should not be surprised at this, from the products of an institution which could put up signs like this:

NO CHARS-A-BANC ALLOWED HERE

or which, possessing over fifty libraries (as at Oxford), could have varying cataloguing systems from each to each, and even within the *same* library!

Oxbridge *can* be debunked, to its consternation. This is usually done by Americans, and some Oxbrites do not mind relating instances of this – *but normally only to other Oxbrites*. It would not do to relax too much in the company of outsiders. Two American tourists, a father and son, once penetrated Exeter College Fellows' Garden. The son romped on the grass (forbidden), while Pop took photos. Observing all this with fury, the Rector stood at his window puffing at his pipe, but disinclined to descend to the vulgarity of yelling at them. Suddenly the Awful Child noticed the don, and shouted to his father, 'Hey, Pop, these ruins are inhabited!'

The boot, however, is more often than not on the other foot:

> US TOURIST: Heck, I can't tell the difference between Lincoln and Jesus.
> OXBRITE: No American can.

As putters-down, few can surpass Oxbrites, and it is a gentle art which must be learnt if one is to survive. A Rhodes scholar, having triumphantly collected a First, was congratulated by his tutor with the words, 'I think you are going to be very influential in thirty years' time.' Once when Robert Morley was being condescending and rude in judging a 'Cuppers' drama production, the safety curtain was 'accidentally' lowered upon him (to sequester, not to damage).

One of the best-remembered local undergraduate bands in Oxford in the early sixties was 'Leon and the Trots', and the Oxbrite of that generation should not only be aware of its name, but of the fact that the Tory Gridiron Club once booked it for a party – apparently unaware of the significance of its name. Similar linguistic gaffes delight Oxbrites: there is the story of the wife of a Warden of New College who was particularly proud of an ancient and valuable Italian chest in her possession:

> WARDEN'S WIFE: Would you like to see my chest?
> CAUTIOUS DON: Only in the presence of your husband.
> WARDEN'S WIFE: (*Looks blank*)

Stories of sit-ins abound, although political activism at Oxbridge has abated greatly since the wave crested in 1968 – 'Avoid joining the Communist Party, at least until after you've been accepted. Dons still remember, with pain, the Cambridge of three or four years ago when sit-ins and demonstrations were regular features of the term. Politics is probably your only problem area – the less you have, the better.' (Undergraduate Advice to Freshers, 1976.) Oxford Oxbrites now in their mid-thirties still remember the sit-in at the Clarendon Building – where, to everyone's disappointment, no secret papers were found. Student unrest of the time, however, led to the interesting spectacle of Marxist undergraduates *insisting* that All Souls fellows did their job of praying – so that at least they should be seen to be doing *something*! In 1968 at Cambridge, the Senate House was occupied, and in 1972 there was a famous sit-in at Old Schools, whose success was marred by a lack of lavatories.

The greatest protest of all happened almost accidentally, but it has attained mythical qualities and is still mentioned with awe by the current generation of Oxbrite undergraduates. It occurred in February 1970 – on Friday 13th, to be exact. The Greek Tourist Office had been celebrating a Greek Week in Cambridge, to drum up tourism for that country, then in the power of the late and unlamented 'Colonels'. On Friday 13th there was to be a junket at the Garden House Hotel, and the *1/- Paper* publicized it thus:

GREEK FASCISTS HOLD A PROPAGANDA PARTY
ALL INVITED
7.30 P.M. FRIDAY 13TH
GARDEN HOUSE HOTEL

Some 350 students turned up. The intention was to picket arriving guests and to listen to a speech by Marcus Dragoumis, an exiled Greek Deputy of one of the centre left parties. A loudspeaker had been set up for Dragoumis outside the hotel, but its power had been cut. It was freezing cold, and the waiting Oxbrites grew restless. They moved around to the back of the hotel and did nothing more violent than drum on the dining room windows, and chant slogans. No Greek-supporting guests were yet even in the dining room. By this time, however, hotel staff were panicking. They called the police, and then the managing director of the hotel and a member of staff turned a fire hose onto the demonstrators from an upstairs window.

The police duly arrived and did a good job of over-reaction, enlivening the old maxim that violence breeds violence. Several undergraduates were arrested (one was charged with having an offensive weapon: in the excitement he had picked up a switch from a bush), and at Colchester Assize they had the misfortune to come before Mr Justice Melford-Stevenson, a hanging judge if ever there was one, and who, it was rumoured among Oxbrites, lived in a house called 'Truncheons'. He sent six Oxbrites to prison, with sentences ranging from between nine and eighteen months, and two to Borstal. For good measure he said that the sentences would have been heavier had it not been for 'the evil influence of some senior members of the university' – a sideswipe at some King's dons whom he had seen as witnesses. Several professors expressed their resentment of his remarks in a letter to *The Times*.

The brutal mishandling by the civil authorities of the whole affair drove a new split between Oxbrites and the police, especially, which has not healed yet, and Melford-Stevenson will be remembered as a man responsible for more social damage than a whole decade of demonstrations. However, as we have seen, since mediaeval times Oxbrites have been more than capable of surviving punch-ups with all-comers. Two years after the 'Garden House Riot', the hotel burnt down. From its ashes a new, expensive Garden House has risen, all black slate and green neon. My spies tell me that it is owned by Trinity.

*   *   *

Dressing up as someone important is very much an Oxbridge thing to do. At about the turn of the century, the Mayor of Cambridge fell for a visit from the Sultan of Zanzibar:

> We collected two friends from Cambridge and another from Oxford, went to London, and got made up at a theatrical costumier's. From London we took the train back to Cambridge, first sending off a telegram to the Mayor warning him to expect us. We signed the telegram 'Lucas', I remember, simply because someone said that high colonial officials always bore that name.
>
> Anyhow, everything went off perfectly. We were met at the station by the Town Clerk and driven in a carriage to the Guildhall, where we were formally received by the Mayor. We then paid a royal visit to a charity bazaar which was going on there, Cole as the Sultan's uncle making enormous purchases at all the stalls, and then emerged into the town, where we were shown the principal colleges.
>
> When all was over, the Town Clerk conducted us back to the station, and then arose the problem of escape . . . as soon as we reached the platform we lifted our skirts, fled through the crowds waiting for the train, jumped into hansoms, and drove off. We just told the cabbies to drive for all they were worth . . .

The famous have found Cambridge just too much, in one way or another. Erasmus wrote to a friend: 'I cannot go out of doors because of the plague . . . I am beset with thieves, and the wine is no better than vinegar . . . I do not like the ale of this place at all . . . My expenses here are enormous; the profits not a brass farthing.' Lytton Strachey said dismally, 'After Cambridge, blank, blank, blank', and Bertrand Russell wrote, 'My first experience of the place was in December 1889 when I was examined for entrance scholarships. I stayed in rooms in the New Court and I was too shy to enquire the way to the lavatory, so that I walked every morning to the station (about $2\frac{1}{2}$ miles there and back) before the examinations began. I

184

wrote to a friend

saw the Backs through the gate of New Court but did not venture to go into them, fearing that they might be private . . .'

There was no need to be intimidated: 'When my uncle, Sir Arthur Shipley, was Vice-Chancellor, a candidate of the same name was presented (for his degree). Instead of "auctoritate mihi commissa admitto te ad gradum baccaulaurei in artibus in nomine Patris et Filii et Spiritus Sancti", he was left wondering if he had really received a degree on hearing the rhythmical intonation of "I-didn't-know-there-was-another-man-in-the-university-called-Shipley, - come - to - lunch - with - me - tomorrow - at -

Christ's-Lodge-at-one-fifteen." ' Vice-Chancellors aren't the only people who needn't be intimidating, either. Even porters often only seem to be. At Clare once a Korean undergraduate called Pin Chuan Ho presented himself at the lodge. 'What's your name?' asked the porter, checking his list. 'Ho,' said the undergraduate. 'Ho's not a name,' said the porter (quick as a flash), it's a staircase.'[1]

Oxford/Cambridge rivalry is not as fierce as it is reputed to be, or as it once was, but Cambridge Oxbrites will be pleased to have at least this squib to let off: Abba Eban, when he was Foreign Secretary of Israel, was congratulated by someone on his Oxford accent. He replied, 'Sir, I would have you know that I went to Cambridge – but in public life you must expect to be smeared.'

What all Oxbrites are joined together in is the difficulty of paying bills (or battels). One Oxbrite at St Catharine's approached this with especial élan. He had already run up a bill at the college buttery (or general store) for £350, and he got a letter from the Domestic Bursar saying that if he didn't settle it by the end of the week he would be allowed no further credit. As it was then Thursday, the Oxbrite wasted no time, and bought on credit from the buttery two cases of Scotch and 2,000 cigarettes. He is now the owner of an international trucking company specializing in transporting pop groups' equipment.

Rivalry apart, too, Oxbrites need not be over-proud of their universities' past reputations. In 1833, when the university was still running the city of Cambridge, the Report of an Enquiry of the Municipal Corporations Committee found that 'probably no judicial investigation into a public trust ever brought to life (*sic*) more shameless profligacy or more inveterate dishonesty, more bare-faced venality in politics, a more heartless disregard of the claims of the poor in the perversion of funds left for their

[1] All staircases are signified by letters of the alphabet.

benefit, or a more degrading subservience to the views of the rich when they appeared in the shape of patrons or distributors of places, a more insatiable cupidity in the corporate officers to enrich themselves with the corporate property, or a more entire neglect of their duties and functions as magistrates, than are presented by the evidence now before us.'

Cambridge, like Oxford, never welcomed interference of any kind from outsiders. In 1851 Sunday excursions to Cambridge were proposed by the Great Eastern Railway, provoking a horrified Vice-Chancellor to comment, 'They have made arrangements for conveying foreigners and others to Cambridge at such fares as might be likely to tempt persons who, having no regard for Sunday themselves, would inflict their presence on the university on that day of rest . . . The contemplated arrangements were as distasteful to the university authorities as they must be to Almighty God and to all right-minded Christians.' Alas, this did not prevent the influx of Common Wickedness. The district of Barnwell had by the end of the nineteenth century become *so* wicked that the Post Office didn't stamp its name on letters posted in it.

All this moved around in the undergrowth, though. In the early sixties, as older Cambridge Oxbrites will remember, an Austin Seven appeared 85 feet up on the Senate House roof. The perpetrators of this prank had dismantled some scaffolding on a nearby building site to construct a derrick to hoist the vehicle to the roof. They then reassembled the scaffolding. It took them three and a half hours in the middle of the night to do. The authorities couldn't get it down in a day. In the end they had to cut it up *in situ*, and lower it in sections. In 1963 a Mini was brought up the Cam on four punts and slung beneath St John's 'Bridge of Sighs'. In the winter of the same year the river froze solid. You could cycle to Grantchester on it, and they roasted a pig on it outside the Garden House

Hotel. Sixties Oxbrites will also remember the 'Peace in Vietnam' banner strung across the top of King's College Chapel. This was also the time of a famous undergraduate whom we will call 'C'. 'C' started his career by being found asleep in his bed in the middle of John's New Court one morning by the porters. He had been carried out there by his friends in the night and left, dead drunk, to his fate. When awakened it wasn't until he had got up and was searching for his slippers with his feet that he noticed that he was touching grass. This story is *so* Oxbridge that it may be regarded as archetypal. On another occasion 'C' climbed to the top of the Cripps Building and played 'Amazing Grace' on his alto saxophone. He was finally restrained as it was 4 a.m.

'C's' greatest coup, however – and also much quoted as an *Oxford* story – was to send a circular to all freshmen requesting them to leave a urine sample in a labelled milk bottle outside the Sister's room. In a porter's version of this story, the attempt is foiled by a perceptive porter who notices that on the circular the word 'nurse' has been used in place of the official 'sister'. Another story which has passed into the mythology of Oxbridge is that of the Chamber Pot cemented to the Chapel Roof. In the Cambridge version, the pot was cemented to one of the pinnacles of King's College Chapel, and they had to get a university marksman to come along and shoot it off.

Older Oxbrites will frequently take pleasure in reminiscing about plumbing. In the fifties, bathrooms at Caius were so awful that undergraduates never used them; and a decade later those in Clare Memorial Court (Mem. Court) were so arranged that a large metal shower rose hung above the bath. In winter, water would condense on this and fall in freezing droplets onto the Oxbrite soaping himself beneath. At Hertford, a fresher asked the porter where the nearest loo to 'F' staircase was. 'Through that quad there, sir, then across the next, then take the third doorway on your right . . .' and so on. After several attempts at establishing whether this loo was indeed the closest (and getting increasingly desperate as he did so), the fresher winkled out the grudging confession, 'There *is* only one, sir.'

Oxbrites coming from the older public schools found all this perfectly normal, as we have seen. What they find less easy to get used to is members of the 'lower orders', to whom they have not been exposed before. One such was flattered by the attention paid him by fellow Trinity men who had come up from Eton, until he was disabused by the sister of one of them: 'Ah, well, you see, whenever they get accused of not knowing any working-class people they all immediately cite you as an example.'

Armed with the information provided above, the would-be Oxbrite will be able to hold his own in Oxbridge circles; it will have done nothing to convince the non-Oxbrites of anything other than the truth of a little poem by Frances Cornford (cousin of Gwen Raverat and third wife of Francis Cornford, the author of *Microcosmographia Academica*) entitled 'Youth':

> A young Apollo, golden-haired,
>   Stands dreaming on the verge of strife,
> Magnificently unprepared
>   For the long littleness of life.

The fact that life would be a good deal more pleasant if everyone could live it as Oxbridge undergraduates (at their happiest) do presents a problem that no one seems to have been able to solve.

[16]

Life After Oxbridge

COMMONLY KNOWN AS 'Poxbridge', an abbreviation of 'post-Oxbridge', this cannot be avoided, even by staying on as an academic – if they'll have you. Some Oxbrites simply cannot let go, and find themselves menial jobs in the town, just to be close to the old Alma Mater. But It Is Never The Same, because it is like living on into extreme old age after all your friends have died. The party has indeed moved on. The average Oxbrite used to think that the world owed him a living, and was often disappointed to find that it did not. Into every Oxbrite has been inculcated a need to question and analyse everything which confronts him, and that need remains with him for life, but only fellow Oxbrites sympathize with it. The would-be Oxbrite can easily emulate this so long as he can penetrate a circle of feeling where there is always a shared sense of conversation, and a desire either to do reckless battle with life and prove yourself (the competitive strain), or a desire to retreat from it and go on reading Rupert Bear, and listening to *The Archers* in a condescending way (the intellectual strain). The two strains co-exist in most Oxbrites, and often conflict. Which makes life very difficult for them.

Young Oxbrites, who really have to fight to get a job, are mercifully free of all this hesitancy and self-indulgence, but sixties and early seventies Oxbrites, who graduated before the advent of Techno-Britain, couldn't get geared up to the reality of looking for work. Most of these were miserable in their first year or so after leaving the academic womb, and some have remained miserable ever since. The confident sense of freedom is over, and can only ever be regained, in a temporary way, in the company of fellow Oxbrites now and then. The amateurish flirtation with the World Outside, which seemed so attractive to indulge in from within the cocoon, is now a marriage, like it or not, and there can be no question of a divorce. Some Oxbrites were so arrogant at their first job interviews that they didn't bother to do a scrap of research beforehand – and were dismayed when they failed. For some it was the first time failure had ever happened to them.

The problem really was this: up until the end of the sixties, Oxbrites were still being turned out in the old-style, gentlemanly mould, equipped for Life rather than for anything so vulgar as a career. At the time, too, you could still walk into many jobs just on the strength of having an Oxbridge degree, regardless of how good it was or what it was in (unless you were a scientist). A First was a passport to success, unless you really mucked things up. The along came Job Experience, Career Loyalty and other unpleasant things. Now, the reality of the seventies and the eighties has baffled Oxbridge. The universities are attempting to cast their charges in the redbrick moulds of Techno-Britain – but the urge to civilize is still stronger than the urge to train, so that success has only been partial. Younger Oxbrites should therefore be warned by the example of the several rootless people in their mid-to-late thirties who drift around Great Britain in sweaters and cords (or Indian dresses – though women tend to be more adaptable, and better at camouflage) – still questioning (if their minds are still functioning) the Purpose of It All. These dangerous and antisocial leftovers are almost certainly the product of sixties Oxbridge.

More hopefully, the completed Oxbrite comes off the production line equipped with a positive drive, too. Place

drift around Great Britain

him at work with an Oxbridge contemporary and all the old competitive instinct will rise again. The boss becomes the tutor or supervisor who has to be pleased or placated. The intelligent manager will employ a bevy of Oxbrites and play them off against each other in this way. An especially successful example of this may be seen in all branches of the Media, to which arts Oxbrites flock like lemmings to a cliff.

From the job-seeking Oxbrites' point of view, the

Oxbridge connection is only valuable up to the age of 25 or so; if they haven't got one by then, they're on the shelf; and if they want to *change* jobs, their Prospective New Employer will be more interested in their career experience. How to play the Oxbridge connection depends very much on whether the PNE is himself Oxbridge or not. If he is, you can, to a certain extent, relax (but be careful: all Oxbrites are fickle, too). If not, one good ploy which has been practised with success is the 'up from nothing' technique: become enthusiastic, allow a Cockney or regional accent to break through your Oxbridge one, and then blush furiously. The PNE will smile: he will think that he has been put at an advantage, and that you are Common Clay like him after all – but by diligence and hard work you have got yourself to and through Oxbridge; something to be applauded.

The Oxbridge 'mafia' is something to be reckoned with, too. It is especially prevalent in broadcasting and publishing, with fingers in journalism and the theatre. In politics an Oxbridge background can be as much a hindrance as a help these days, and scientists don't seem to care much about the Oxbridge connection either way. Once 'in' the Oxbridge mafia, however, Oxbrites need not think that they can relax. They must continue to impress and/or compete with their peers, because just like Cosa Nostra, the Oxbridge mafia likes to keep its standards high. On another level, it is simply recreating the neurotic competitiveness all Oxbrites learn at Oxford and carry with them to the grave. Would-be Oxbrites should pick their career and university carefully. Broadly speaking, the arts world cares most about an Oxbridge background, and a general table of who takes what from where may be summarized as follows:

OXFORD	OXBRIDGE	CAMBRIDGE
Art critics	Civil Servants	Account Execu-
Literary agents	Diplomats	tives (rare)
Novelists	The Law[1]	Actors
Philosophers	MI5/MI6	Administrators
Playwrights	Scientists	Copywriters
Poets		Documentary
Politicians		Film-makers
Publishers (women)		Film critics
tv arts programme-		Political journalists
makers/presenters		Publishers (men)
tv directors		Theatre directors
		tv journalists
		tv producers

An irony of the job rat race is encapsulated in the following event, which occurred at a television station run at the time by Oxbrites for the benefit of the lower orders. 'We must go downmarket,' the Management liberally decided. Late one night a short time afterwards, three Oxbrites were agonizing over a script for an item, which they were typing into the company computer (a machine whose subtleties none of them fully grasped anyway, since they were all arts Oxbrites and really expected to have menials to operate it for them):

> OXBRITE 'A' (MA *English*): Shall we say, 'And now let's take a look at the whacky world of advertising'?
>
> OXBRITE 'B' (Ph. D. *History*): Wouldn't it be better to say, 'And now let's go behind the scenes …'?
>
> OXBRITE 'C' (B. Phil. *English*): No. Too literary. 'And

---

[1] Note that Oxbrites do not become policemen and thus follow a profession which pursues criminals, but they become barristers and follow a profession which gets criminals off. The perverseness is typical.

now, let's take a *peek* at the *crazy* world of advertising ...'

OXBRITE 'A' (*Fretfully*): 'Peek' sounds dated. Doesn't
it?

OXBRITE 'C': All right. How about: 'And now, have
you ever wondered what makes those zany ad-men
tick'?

(*At this point all three start giggling.*)

OXBRITE 'B' (*Recovering*): For Christ's sake let's get
this over with and go and have a drink. It's nearly
eleven.

THE EDITOR (*Also Oxbrite:* MA *History; approaching
nervously and reading what there is of the script*): No, no
this won't do. They'll think we're sending them up.

It is interesting to see how wildly Oxbrites scrabble to
get into the media, only to have to throw their three years'
expensive education onto the scrap-heap. Who cares now
if you know all about the symbolism of the stage-
directions in *Rosmersholm*? On the other hand, the notional
attraction of all that money, and power over what other
people think, is probably what has spurred them on.
Oxbrites are basically grasping and vain, just like everybody else!

Very few painters, musicians and dancers are Oxbridge. And very few Oxbrites get the kind of career
springboard which one did as recently as 1982. A Trinity
racing bore, who was always offering notoriously bad tips,
went down with a Third and No Prospects. Some time
later he was gloomily at the Curragh, and recklessly gave
a 'hot' tip to an Irish businessman there. The Irishman
put £5,000 on the horse, which came in first at 33:1. Our
Hero was rewarded with a £25,000 a year job with a
pharmaceutical company in Africa.

Marriage presents a different set of problems to the Oxbrite. We have seen that few inter-Oxbrite partnerships last, and those Oxbrites who avoid matrimony in the early stages either succeed in doing so altogether, or leave it as long as possible, until loneliness or the need for cash drives them to it. This avoidance of 'setting up home' derives less from aversion to the idea than to the time-honoured Oxbrite custom of dithering a lot before committing oneself. Once decided, however, the Oxbrite will often recklessly plunge – which may be one factor accounting for the high divorce rate among Oxbrites. Another, of course, is the practice of drinking too much and talking too much instead of Going To Bed.

One general rule is that Oxbrites are better off with non-Oxbrites. Otherwise the whole thing gets far too in-bred. Partnership with a non-Oxbrite also carries certain other advantages. The non-Oxbrite spouse will never fail, if you play your cards right, to think you far more intelligent than you in fact are, and will treat you with according deference and care. This can be especially soothing to the Oxbridge ego, returning home perhaps after a battering day at the office, and requires little effort on the Oxbrite's part. It is a mistake for the Oxbrite to assume, however, that he need put no more into his marriage (or she into hers) than the opportunity to bask in the reflected glory of three years' education a long time ago; and if he or she harps on the Oxbridge connection too much, particularly in the context of a marriage to a totally uneducated non-Oxbrite, tension can ensue. In this as in all matters, once you have established your Oxbridgidity, there is no need to emphasize it any more. It will be self-maintaining.

In the early stages of a serious courtship, the Oxbrite is at a distinct advantage with his future in-laws, if he does not drink and talk too much, and always provided that they are not themselves Oxbridge. A good example of this is the case of an unsuccessful 'writer' who was hoping to get hitched to the daughter of a wealthy ex-Brigadier. The fact that the Oxbrite was half-German put him at a further disadvantage. He approached his potential in-laws in their Surrey fastness with trepidation, having no career, no money and no prospects. *But he had been to Oxford.* The imprimatur of respectability was thus upon him, and his way to the altar smoothed.

There are times, of course, when the premise opposite to that put forward in this book applies, and true Oxbrites find themselves obliged to pretend that they are *non*-Oxbrite to gain their ends. This can occur equally in the hunt for a job, and the hunt for a partner. In the job circumstance, it is useful if confronted with a prospective employer who is Bluff, and From the Midlands, or for any Oxbrite seeking a future in ball-bearings or sports journalism. In the marriage stakes, it is useful if you encounter a possible father-in-law of the 'I've studied at the university of life' type. Instinct will tell you how to play your cards, and the golden rule is, never show them until you have to, and *never boast*. As we have already suggested, Oxbrites are so sure of their own superiority that they do not need to. Big powerful cars, big powerful dogs, and big powerful people are always the quietest.

Since society has been saddled with the expression 'Oxford accent', passing reference should be made to the advantages and disadvantages of accents which are not 'Oxford', now that the possession of one no longer provides the automatic entrée to society that it used to (in some cases it is to be avoided or disguised – see the preceding paragraph).

As a rule of thumb, guidelines for accent are the same as for where it is best to live (see below), but in both cases *the sand can shift*, so be warned. A slight Liverpool or general Northern or Yorkshire burr, charming and bankable ten to twenty years ago, is now an embarrassing encumbrance; whereas a *Cockney* accent nowadays will get you in just about anywhere. West of England accents always evince the traditional expectation of yokeldom and slowness, so avoid them – although in non-feminist Oxbrites with little ambition they can be attractive. *Southern* Irish has a certain pull, used judiciously. *Northern* Irish and most country and Glasgow *Scottish* accents, despite all the efforts of the BBC, have none, and nor under any circumstances do Lancashire or Midlands voices. Avoid Welsh accents like the plague if you are male, though female Oxbrites will find that a lightly applied *northern* Welsh accent will unlock the odd door. If you have not been born with a favourable accent, adopt one, but make sure that it comes easily to you, and that you like it, as you will be stuck with it for a long time. Do not 'adopt' an accent at all if you talk in your sleep.

Life after Oxbridge usually means finding somewhere else to live. Most career-minded arts Oxbrites gravitate inevitably to London, but London has the qualities of a country in itself, with its own *in* and *out* areas for the Oxbrite. Depending on your role in life, you can take it that it will always be acceptable to live in Bath, Bristol, Durham, Edinburgh, York, Norfolk, Suffolk, anywhere in central London *north* of the river (especially Islington), but only *south* of the river in Battersea, Camberwell, Clapham and Wandsworth; and most places in the safer Home Counties like Surrey, Sussex, Hampshire and Berkshire. Conversely, it will never be acceptable in Oxbridge circles to move to Huddersfield, Penge, Sidcup, Welshpool, anywhere in the West Midlands or Northern Ireland, and anywhere in central London *south* of the river except those places mentioned above. Other areas of the UK, and everywhere abroad (except for *out* regions such as Belgium, Central and South America, South Africa and the midwestern USA) may be regarded as neutral zones, although certain places with obvious cachet such as Amsterdam, Paris, New York, San Francisco and Moscow (for older Oxbrites) may be considered *in*.

There follows the question of interior décor. The Oxbrite is used to:

(a) the parental home
(b) furnished rooms in college
(c) squalid digs.

His choice of house or flat will depend entirely upon where he lives and what he can afford, but for preference it will be (a) spacious, and (b) old. Spacious, because Oxbrites are untidy and messy and, if they are living with someone else, often feel the need to be alone. Old, because Oxbrites like places with thick walls so that the noise transmitted to or received from neighbours will be as muffled as possible. However, Oxbrites are not, by and large, materialistic, except where the possession can be a means of demonstrating to other Oxbrites how well they have 'got on', and so they do not *much* mind what they live in, or what they wear, but they *do* care about where they live (the snob appeal of a good postal area in London, for example), and what they drive (although they pretend not to).

Home in post-Oxbridge life will reflect the décor of his undergraduate years – the more so if he remains unmarried. A famous mediaperson known to the author lived for many years in a mansion flat in Hampstead. Most of the rooms were ascetic to the point of being spartan, but the largest room was a replica of the sort an undergraduate Oxbrite has in college, comprising as it did bedsitting room and study. The chimney-piece was stacked with Invitations, the desk was piled with books, *Guardians*, *Timeses*, bits of paper and an old Olivetti; you couldn't see the walls for untidy bookshelves, and – crowning glory – above the rumpled bed an oar was hung. The interior of married Oxbrites' houses will vary according to how far their own taste has been watered down or suppressed by their partners, but most will retain the following features:

(a) a Toulouse-Lautrec reproduction poster in the loo;
(b) a large number of untidy but well-read paperbacks, among them plenty with blue, black or grey spines – some of the thicker ones bought 10–15 years ago and still in pristine condition
(c) a pile of old *Private Eyes*;
(d) pine furniture;
(e) dark wall colours.

Sixties Oxbrites will also have a dusty pile of records by people like Nina Simone, Leonard Cohen, the Rolling Stones, Velvet Underground and the Incredible String Band – the Beatles were considered too tame by many Oxbrites – as well as a paperback containing all the lyrics of Bob Dylan's songs, which they will know bits of by heart, though they will not quote them nowadays with quite such hollow-eyed awe at their significance as they used to. Oxbrites are not keen do-it-yourselfers, and many of them have little or no sense of taste in interior décor. David Hicks would mean nothing to most of them, and they wouldn't even flinch at the sight of an Ercol sofa. The only thing which might offend them is clashing patterns, about which they would be merciless. They themselves go for plain colours, but if there is a pattern it will be a classic, or will reflect the prevailing fashion of the time when they were undergraduates; Oxbrites in their thirties have a lot of William Morris repro. and Laura Ashley stuff about the place. Bare wood is greatly favoured, and although ornaments tend to be avoided, there will be a few self-consciously juvenile things – a shelf-full of Asterix books (in French, of course), an air pistol, a doll, a teddy-bear and a couple of old Dinky toys. No Oxbrite home is complete without a copy of *Winnie-the-Pooh* (though many Oxbrites can't cope with *The House At Pooh Corner* because it Faces Reality at the end) and *The Wind In The Willows*. Older Oxbrites will have the complete works of Tolkien buried somewhere as well. Kids' things are important to all Oxbrites, because they all like to delay maturity for as long as possible.

Oxbrites dress in very much the same way as they decorate their homes: either classically or, more frequently, in the fashion prevailing when they were undergraduates. They are more interested in clothes than they are in interior décor, and some are quite dandified in youth, although paradoxically they are not deeply interested in fashion, feeling that on the whole their minds should be on higher things. High fashion is even deemed faintly vulgar by female Oxbrites, who remain faithful to the 'midi', Laura Ashley and Indian cotton print if they are over 30. If they are over 30 and rich and single, and work as, say, television producers, they will go either for a masculine look – jeans and a leather bomber jacket (but from Fiorucci), or for the well-tailored elegance of Roland Klein or Jasper Conran (sample sales are cheaper, but you have to get on the mailing list); if you *must* go to a store, go to Harvey Nichols; buy your trousers from Céline's and your shoes from Charles Jourdan. Beauchamp Place and Bond Street will supply every other need. The keynote as always must be understatement. Oxbrites avoid anything which has the maker's name wrought into it as a pattern, or which has any kind of distinctive 'house' pattern. They never wear T-shirts or sweaters with the maker's name or any message emblazoned on them, and wouldn't be seen dead in pullovers with things like 'Guinness' or 'Malibu' written across their chests. A true Oxbrite wouldn't know what Malibu was.

The only time when overstatement (i.e. fun) is allowed is in clothing that no one else sees (except a spouse, or a lover who can be trusted). I know a respectable young QC who habitually wears gold and mauve floral pyjamas; a schoolteacher in Manchester who favours black leather baby doll nightdresses (strictly for her own amusement), and a priest in Los Angeles who has seven different floor-length silk dressing gowns, each in an electric shade of one of the colours of the spectrum.

Underwear, tights and socks all come from Marks and Spencer, like everyone else's.

Male Oxbrites tend to have to wear suits, like ordinary mortals, if they work in offices, politics, the Civil Service or the diplomatic corps. However, they generally manage to look scruffy even in an expensive suit, and they tend to have haircuts only half as often as they should. In the arty professions, the male Oxbrite clings to the brown bomber-jacket-and-blue-jeans look of his youth, often accompanied by an appalling neckscarf with loud colours – for example, turquoise and orange. He will wear such clothes until well into his late thirties (unless he has a wife to put him right), when the incipient paunch brought on by far too much gin, scotch, wine and cognac (the post-Oxbridge Oxbrite is not an habitual beer-drinker) begins to make him look like a large toffee apple on a blue stick.

Corduroy also plays an exaggerated role in the male Oxbridge wardrobe.

Both sexes relax in pullovers-and-jeans. Upmarket Oxbrites wear guernseys *but only dark blue ones*. You will still see the British Heavy Leather Sandal on a variety of Oxbridge feet in the summer.

For the wearing of college and club ties, see above, Chapter 10. If in doubt, do *not* wear them.

Transport presents a good many problems for Oxbrites. For one thing, they have to affect not to be interested in such a boring thing as a car (unless they are scientists); for another they have to deal with the inverted snobbery of other Oxbrites, who may be as rich as Croesus but who drive old bangers, to show their contempt for:

(a) the car as a status symbol
(b) the *hoi polloi* who *use* the car as a status symbol.

Among Oxbrites, then, the principle of judging how well people have 'got on' by the car they drive is obfuscated. It is further complicated by the fact that many Oxbrites do actually love cars, and are able in unguarded moments to become quite enthusiastic in pub conversations about such simple motoristic issues as 'automatic versus gears' (they are not mechanics and so cannot tackle really heavy subjects); indeed, many Oxbrites would buy the shiniest and fastest thing on four wheels, *if they could afford it*. As we have seen, though, Oxbrites are not usually successful in business. They envy self-made people, but consider them, and the whole operation of making money, vulgar. In fact they could not do it if they tried because they will always talk rather than act, and dither rather than be decisive. Thus most Oxbrites (especially male ones) are poor.

The archetypal Oxbrite, then, would love to drive a Bentley but actually drives a Renault 4. No Oxbrites, of course, look after their car (that would show a dangerous and unintellectual inclination to be practical), and so it should be so dirty (inside and out) as for its colour to be almost indistinguishable; the neglected engine should choke and roar; the gears should grind and, most important of all, the car should be *at least five years old, but no more than ten*. Newer than five is flashy and vulgar; older than ten is either an indication of *real* poverty (i.e. failure), or eccentricity (i.e. covering up for failure). Oxbrites would love to have a company car, but as the jobs they do generally don't provide them, they sneer at those who do. Very rarely, Oxbrites will come out of the closet and buy themselves a red Ferrari, but such persons have clearly ceased to care what being an Oxbrite is all about.

Some Oxbrites go to the other extreme, talk loudly

about petrol, and world pollution, and travel by public transport. Some even walk. Very few revert to the bicycle, despite the current fashion for that dangerous machine.

If Oxbrites marry and do not hold theories about the overpopulation of the planet (i.e. are rich enough), and if they do not drink too much and talk too much, it is a fair bet that sooner or later they will produce children. These will be the same as any other children, but Oxbridge parents will want the child to grow up to be an Oxbrite too, thereby committing themselves to fifteen years of anxious waiting. The second problem is the Name. This should be decided upon immediately by sticking a pin in a book, naming the infant after a famous, or rich, but elderly relative, or settling the whole thing well in advance and adhering rigidly to the decision, once made. If none of these courses is taken, the discussion will take so long that the child could well end up anonymous. I do not propose to offer any kind of helpful list here because there are no hard and fast rules governing the naming of Oxbridge children (indeed Oxbrites quite often revert to their old pre-Oxbridge personae when it comes to this task, and are quite untypically their naked selves for a moment), but the astute Oxbrite will not saddle his heirs with names that

(a) are currently very fashionable (By your name shall ye be dated. Look at the wave of Susans, Rosemarys and Annes that hit the country around 1952, and the vast number of Charleses *c.* 1948/49. Other examples are many and obvious. Royalty and Film Stars are responsible, and should keep their names secret, or use special ones. God knows how many Dis, Williams and Harrys there are coming up)

(b) can be abbreviated to silly nicknames (e.g. Sebastian – Seb)

(c) are so arty that the child will grow up to loathe you (e.g. Tamarisk, Inigo)

(d) lead to inappropriate initials (e.g. Sarah Anne Gladstone)

(e) reflect bad good taste (e.g. Tristram, Hermia).

Instead he will go for classical evergreens like Anthony and Elizabeth, Christopher and Louise. If he *must* be arty or trendy, he will in any case studiously avoid Damon and Jason, Tracey and Sharon, and he will avoid common names like Les, Dave or Ron – although, of course, Leslie (though *not* Lesley), David and Ronald (just) are fine. Equally the Oxbrite will dislike 'upper' names like Henry or Georgina – and Charles and Caroline have been vulgarized by over-use. Some sixties Oxbridge parents made the terrible mistake of going for names like Moonlight, Dreamer and Skyfox – the wretched 20-year-olds who bear them have by now, of course, buried them.

Many Oxbrites give their children Beatrix Potter crockery to eat off.

The family circle is completed by pets, which are optional. One or two simple rules apply here: no Oxbrite would ever keep goldfish or budgerigars; and Oxbrites tend to be 'cat' people rather than 'dog' people. This is partly because cats require very little maintenance; for the same reason no Oxbrite would have a *pedigree* cat. Pet snobbery doesn't exist for Oxbrites, so that even if they own a dog it can be any old mutt. However, the Oxbrites' intellectual snobbery often comes out in the way they *name* their pets. If they have shown restraint in naming their children they throw it to the winds when naming their pets, and dumb animals (especially cats, which don't have to be called in public as often as dogs) are saddled with the wildest pieces of eccentricity and pretentiousness. (NB: The craze for giving your animal a 'common' name, like Fred, or Pete, is *over*. It is still permissible perversely to give your pet a name usually reserved for humans, e.g. Philip; Mary.)

'Pushkin' is common for a cat; but what about having two, and calling them 'Stuff' and 'Nonsense'? One Oxbrite, returning to London after a year's exile in the Midlands, called his black doctored tomcat, which was fat, lazy and smelly, 'Birmingham'. 'Desdemona' and 'Cymbeline', and other of the more rarefied Shakespearean names, abound, along with self-consciously *risqué* ones like 'Lucifer' and 'Lilith'. Cats with classical owners get names like 'Anacreon', 'Aesculapius', and – appallingly – 'Oedi-puss'. Other punning names include 'Muir', and 'Purrfect Pussy', while a certain Dr Hodge of the author's acquaintance called his cat 'Johnson'.

Not all Oxbrites feel the need to belong to a club, but if you *do* join one, the current favourite is the Garrick, which is expensive, exclusive and has a long waiting list; membership of it is therefore an ideal way of showing that you have 'got on'. It also serves good food in splendid and comfortable rooms, and the staff tend to be more friendly than stuffy. The Garrick is the place for the Oxbrite who is in Journalism (*Times* rather than *Sun*), Law and – decreasingly – Theatre. For the politician there is still the Reform Club, and for the cleric the Athenaeum. The one club *no* self-respecting Oxbrite will join is the ailing Oxford and Cambridge, where the members *all* wear their college ties, and a smell of over-cooked cabbage traditionally pervades the place – though my spies inform me that the club is rallying under the guidance of a young cleric called David Johnson.

'The friends you make at Oxbridge are the friends you make for life' is a misconception many older Oxbrites (whom experience should have taught) and non-Oxbrites labour under. Inevitably, on life's stormy seas, you lose contact with most of the ships which left harbour with you. *However*, the Oxbrite nearly always finds that 'the friends you make in life are all, by some remarkable coincidence, from Oxbridge (more or less)'. 'Other people just don't seem quite so reliable, somehow,' as one of my informants told me. 'Knock an Oxbridge man and it's like knocking a piece of solid English oak: *solid*, through and through. But not, of course, as thick.'

Before leaving the subject of clubs and friends, a word should be spoken about 'Gaudies' and 'Reunion Dinners'. A 'Gaudy' (from the Latin, *gaude*) is a college reunion dinner at Oxford (cf. Dorothy L. Sayers' *Gaudy Night*, and J. I. M. Stewart's *The Gaudy*). Old Magdalen men, say, from selected adjacent years (Oxbrites are never lost track of by their colleges, and are dated by the year in which they went up), say, 1937, 1938, 1939, all troop up to Oxford and put on dinner jackets and eat, drink and talk too much in their old Hall. It sounds fun but in fact the most interesting 'old boys' are usually too busy doing interesting things to go back, so that the bore factor is high. Reunion Dinners are the same thing at Cambridge.

Old alumni are kept posted by means of a college 'annual' which brings them up to date with news of other old alumni, and tells them who has 'got on' best, and who has died. Rather wittily, the Clare Association Annual's accompanying form for information has a section entitled: 'NEWS of other Clare members (e.g. items you think they may be unlikely to notify to the College more directly, especially deaths!)'. From such an annual, news of Reunion Dinners can also be gleaned. Old Clare men who went up in 1930, 1931, 1932, 1933 are having one in July 1987, for example. Occasionally the college will write requesting money for some building project or other, for example, the appalling new library with which Clare has defiled Memorial Court.

Finally, in this review of Oxbridge, a note on How to be Remembered is in order. There are three ways to do this

Appendix: '-er' and epigrams

ANCIENT OXBRITES will remember (just) the Oxford habit of slang which involved contorting words so that they ended in '-er'. For example:

bedmaker – bedder*
a cup of cocoa – a cugger of cocoa
epigram – epigragger
freshman – fresher*
football – footer*
the Master – the Magger
rugby football – rugger*
sing song – siggersogger
association football – soccer*
tangerine – tangerigger
tennis – tenner
Torpids – Toggers
wastepaper basket – wagger pagger bagger.

This is turn-of-the-century stuff, and only a few examples (marked with an asterisk) survive.

I should point out here, too, that the habit of coming out with pregnant-sounding epigrams should not be indulged in by Oxbrites under 40, since it is no longer *in*. Four examples of what I mean should suffice:

'What is seriousness? It is merely brilliant fooling.'
'God is a fable, writ in Holy Water.'
'Luck is the name we give to the skill of others.'
'Art is knowing what to leave unsaid.'

By the same token, would-be Oxbrites should never pass themselves off as former Oxbridge eccentrics. These are always few and far between, and are always remembered by genuine Oxbrites.

Glossary

ACADEMIC (*n.* & *adj.*): a fellow or don; a university teacher or general layabout; (*adj.*) appertaining to Oxbridge (questionable elsewhere).

AEGROTAT (*n.*): form of degree granted to Oxbrites too ill to face finals.

ALL-NIGHTER (*n.*): staying up all night to revise or finish the essay that's been put off all week. Involves drinking too much instant coffee and feeling giddy. Best done with a room-mate: then you can stick pins into each other to stay awake.

ALUMNUS/ALUMNA (*n.*): undergraduate (during) and graduate (after) the process of being Oxbridgized.

BA (*n.*): Bachelor of Arts. The commonest sort of degree for an arts or humanities undergraduate to finish on.

BACKS, the (*n.*) (*Cambridge*): that part of the Cam which is lined with colleges. Not to be confused with VACS.

BATTELS (*n.*): (*Oxford*): the dreadful bill at the end of every term.

BEDDER (*n.*): female cleaner and erstwhile supervisor of morals.

BLUE (*n.*): Honour conferred on top Oxbridge sportspersons who go into battle against the other place (q.v.).

BOATER (*n.*): flat-topped straw hat with an oval brim and a hatband in the college colours worn by supporters of rowers, and punting pseuds, and butchers.

BOATIE (*n.*): thuglike rower.

BOD, the (*n.*) (*Oxford*): the Bodleian Library (interior unknown to many Oxbrites).

BROAD, the (*n.*) (*Oxford*): Broad Street. *Via academica.*

B.Sc. (*n.*): Bachelor of Science. The commonest sort of degree for a science undergraduate to finish on.

BULLDOG (*n.*): university policeman. They hunt in pairs, attending a proctor, and providing the muscle to his crocodile courtesy.

BUMPING RACE/BUMPS (*n.*): university local boat races.

BUTTERY (*n.*): college grocery and general store. Everything on tick, but they can be tough creditors in the end.

CAFFEINE POISONING (*n.*): disease endemic among all Oxbrites when undergraduates. Later replaced by alcohol poisoning.

CAMBRIDGE (*n.*) (*Cambridge*): the university, not the town; (*Oxford*): the other place.

CANTAB. (*n.*): abbreviation of Latin *Cantabrigia*, for Cambridge.

CAP (*n.*): 'mortar board', called a 'square' at Cambridge.

CARFAX (*n.*) (*Oxford*): crumbling mediaeval tower which is the notional centre of Oxford.

CHERWELL (*n.*) (*Oxford*): pronounced CHARWELL, it is the name of one of the rivers at Oxford, and the name of the undergraduates' weekly newspaper.

CHEST, University (*n.*) (*Oxford*): where the university boodle is kept.

CLASS (*n.*): sometimes called 'grade' – it's the level of degree you get. Not to be confused with social or school life.

CLERK OF THE MARKET (*n.*) (*Oxford*): 'Privilege conferred on dons of great academic distinction, worth £5 per annum and meaningless today.'

CLERK OF THE UNIVERSITY (*n.*) (*Oxford*): undergraduate.

COG (*n.*): abbr. of 'Cognoscento'; an undergraduate who

is sophisticated and absolutely in the know (rare).

COMBINATION ROOM (*n.*) (*Cambridge*): a sort of clubroom for reading *The Times*, bitching and drinking claret. Dons have one called the SCR (Senior Combination Room), Graduates have one called the M (Middle) CR, and undergraduates have one called the J (Junior) CR.

COME UP (*v.*): what you do when you first arrive, and at the beginning of every term.

COMMON ROOM (*n.*) (*Oxford*): just like the Combination Room at Cambridge.

COMMONER (*n.*) (*Oxford*): the lowest form of undergraduate.

COMMONER

CORN, the (*n.*) (*Oxford*): Cornmarket. Main ordinary shopping drag, used by townies as well.

COURT (*n.*) (*Cambridge*): a (usually) grassed square surrounded by college buildings, within the college.

CREW TABLE, the (*n*): a better class of food for rowers

specially served in Hall (q.v.) to build them up during Torpids, Eights Week, Lents, Mays, etc.

CREWEIAN BENEFACTION, the (*n.*) (*Oxford*): strawberries and champagne for the élite during Encaenia.

CUPPERS (*n.*) (*Cambridge*): sports trials for newcomers; (*Oxford*): arts trials for newcomers, especially theatricals.

DESPERATE (*n.*): one whose sex life is not all it could be.

DON (*n.*): permanent inhabitant of Oxbridge; found in Groves of Academe only. The name comes from the Latin *dominus*=master (or lord).

EASTER (*n.*) (*Cambridge*): summer term.

ECCENTRICITY (*n.*): ploy exercised at Oxbridge to cover lack of confidence, or money.

EIGHTS WEEK (*n.*) (*Oxford*): a lot of Bumps in May.

ENCAENIA (*n.*) (*Oxford*): the ceremony at which everybody dresses up like mad, and honorary degrees are doled out to megastars.

ETYM. DUB. (*adj.*): slightly archaic way of saying 'I don't know', without quite committing yourself.

EXHIBITIONER (*n.*): an undergraduate who is brighter than a commoner or a pensioner, but dimmer than a scholar.

FELLOW (*n.*): a bit like a don, but belonging absolutely to a college.

FINALS (*n.*) (*Cambridge*): probably the last exams you will ever take.

FRESHER/FRESHMAN (*n.*): newly arrived Oxbrite. The name sticks for about as long as his/her first term.

GATED (*p.p.*): not often used or inflicted now, but it means confined to quarters.

GAUDY (*n.*) (*Oxford*): junket in Hall for old boys.

GCM (*n.*) (*Cambridge*): Great Cambridge Mind. A type more often talked about than seen.

GLAD RAGS (*n.*): party clothes, whether formal or not.

GLF (*n.*): Godlike Figure. Minor luminaries on the Oxbridge scene.

GNOME (*n.*) (*Oxford*): one who puts work before pleasure; *sometimes* used as a verb.

GO DOWN (*v.*): what you do at the end of every term, and what you do at the end, provided that you survive the course.

GOM (*n.*): Great Oxford Mind – as for Great Cambridge Mind.

GOWN (*n.*): black, raglike jerkin worn in loose style by undergraduates. Sometimes blue. Grander academic Oxbrites get to wear much glossier numbers in a variety of colours.

GRADBASHING (*n.*): townies' version of beagling.

GRADUAND (*n.*): one who is in the process of graduating. An impermanent state.

GRADUATE (*n.*): one who has stood the course, and can prove it.

GREATS (*n.*) (*Oxford*): the second half of the classics course.

GREY MAN (*n.*) (*Cambridge*): the same as a gnome at Oxford. But *also* a club and party bore.

GROCKLE (*n.*): any non-Oxbrite. Depending on who you are, it can, of course, be an appellation to be proud of.

GYP (*n.*) (*Cambridge*): male college servant. Usually well advanced in years, or of diminished responsibility.

HACK (*n.*): one who pushes him or herself desperately in university societies, usually to be found in its extreme form in university theatre, politics or journalism. The hack hopes to thrive in the World Outside by virtue of his endeavours at Oxbridge.

HALF-BLUE (*n.*): a kingpin sportsman (or woman) in one of the 'lesser' university sports.

HALL (*n.*): dinner. Can be awful, but food is better when the Hall is either 'Formal' or 'Super'. Has to be eaten in the college hall, and clothes must be worn.

HALL'S (*adj.* & *n.*) (*Oxford*): one of the predominating beers.

HEAD OF HOUSE (*n.*): the boss of your college, be he Master, Principal, Warden, Provost or Dean (or whatever).

HEARTIE (*n.*): general sport/theatre/journalistic loud-mouthed sexstarved beerswilling bore.

HEBDOMADAL COUNCIL (*n.*) (*Oxford*): the boys with the real administrative power.

HIGH, the (*n.*) (*Oxford*): High Street. Long and trafficky.

HIGH TABLE (*n.*): where the Fellows sit at Hall. The table is usually raised above the level of the floor, and the food is better, too.

HILARY (*n.*) (*Oxford*): the Easter term.

ISIS (*n.*) (*Oxford*): the other river. Where the local rowing is done. The word is a shortened form of the Latin for the Thames, *Thamesis*, and is nothing to do with the Egyptian goddess, despite a misleading undergraduate magazine called *Osiris* (not to mention *Mesopotamia*).

JCR (*n.*): Junior Combination/Common Room. Where dullish undergraduates swill Nescafé and watch 'Match of the Day'.

KA (*n.*): the King's Arms. Oxford pub noted for its Wadham and erstwhile OUDS connections.

KING'S (*n.*) (*Cambridge*): college noted for brilliance, money, lefties and Gays.

LITTLE GO (*n.*) (*Cambridge*): a defunct common entrance exam.

LITTLEGO (*n.*) (*Oxford*): the same as 'Mods.' – once.

LODGE (*n.*): a very grand house within the college where the Head of House lives, *or* a dingy and overheated gatehouse where the porters work.

LONG VAC (*n.*): long summer 'holiday' from June to October.

LUMINARY (*n.*): the sort of Oxbrite who makes good in public life in the World Outside. To qualify, he must figure at least once a month in the quality Sunday papers.

MA (*n.*): Master of Arts. At Oxbridge, it's simply a matter of degree.

MACHINE, to (*v.*): what Oxbridge undergraduates do when they're practising Machiavellianism.

MAY MORNING (*n.*) (*Oxford*): choral singsong at sparrow's fart on top of Magdalen Tower. Plus Morris dancing and booze. Any excuse will do. This one's the first of May.

MAY WEEK (*n.*) (*Cambridge*): the first two weeks of June. A post-examination junket.

MCR (*n.*): Combination/Common Room for graduates.

MODS (*n.*) (*Oxford*): yet another sort of exam. Not to be confused with the people who used to fight with Rockers.

MORTAR BOARD (*n.*): hard, flat, tasselled cap. Never called this at Oxbridge.

NEWDIGATE PRIZE (*n.*) (*Oxford*): principal university prize for a poem on a set theme.

NEWMAN ROOMS (*n.*) (*Oxford*): dubious meeting place for Roman Catholics.

NERD/NURD (*n.*): twerp.

NOCTIVAGATE (*v.*) (*Archaic*): to go around town, pre-

ferably gownless, after dark. Once upon a time you
could be done by the proctors for doing this.
NORRINGTON TABLE (*n.*) (*Oxford*): league table of
academic success among the colleges.

OTHER PLACE, the (*n.*) (*Cambridge*): Oxford; (*Oxford*):
Cambridge.
OUDS (*n.*) (*Oxford*): the best-known drama club.
OXBRIDGE (*n. & adj.*): the quality and state of being in
or from Oxford or Cambridge universities (or both).
OXBRIDGESE (*n.*): the 'argot' of Oxbridge.
OXBRIDGIDITY (*n.*): the quality possessed by all Ox-
brites.
OXBRITE (*n.*): one who is now, or has ever been, at
Oxbridge.
OXFORD (*n.*) (*Cambridge*): the other place; (*Oxford*): the
university, not the town.
OXON. (*n.*): abbreviation of Latin *Oxonia*, for Oxford.

PENSIONER (*n.*) (*Cambridge*): the lowest form of undergraduate.
Ph.D (*n.*): Doctor of Philosophy. First real step for the
career academic.
PRELIMS (*n.*): more exam types. Beware of the difference between this sort at Cambridge and at Oxford.
PROCTOR (*n.*): academic policeman. Aided by two bulldogs (q.v.) this person's job is to punish you if you
overstep the mark.
PROG (*v.*): now archaic. What a proctor does when he
catches you. Better imagined than described.
POLY DOLLY (*n.*) (*Oxford*): Oxford male Oxbrites don't
care where they get their women from. This refers to a
female student at the Oxford Polytechnic.
PORT MEADOW (*n.*) (*Oxford*): vast expanse of open,
common land to the west of the town. It is put to various
uses, none of which I have room to describe here.

PUNT (*n.* & *v.*): a flat rectangular boat for use on shallow rivers; propulsion of said boat.

QUAD (*n.*) (*Oxford*): the same as a Cambridge court. Short for quadrangle.

RAG TABLE (*n.*): league list of the colleges who collect the most money for charity by dressing up as babies, throwing mud, holding slave markets, etc., during rag week.

READ (*v.*): to study a subject at Oxbridge.

RESPONSIONS (*n.*) (*Oxford*): yet another sort of exam.

RUGGERBUGGER (*n.*): beery, rugby-playing tough. Often violent.

RUSTICATED (*p.p.*): kicked out for anything from a term to a year to cool off. Punishment for minor excesses.

SCHOLAR (*n.*): the brainiest type of undergraduate. Gets paid for it, too.

SCHOOLS (*n.*) (*Oxford*): term used for examinations, more especially final examinations, but also the shortened name for the building where the things are sat.

SCONCE (*v.*): to challenge someone to quaff far too much beer off in one as a result of his breaching Hall etiquette. Now rare.

SCONCING STOUP (*n.*): a kind of large cup often resembling a two-handled chamber pot in silver, used to contain the beer to be drunk off at a sconce.

SCOUT (*n.*) (*Oxford*): male or female college servant, akin to the gyps and bedders of Cambridge. Good relations pay.

SCR (*n.*): Senior Combination/Common Room. This one's for the dons. Claret and Havanas.

SCREENS (*n.*): notice boards which usually run along the corridor separating the Hall from the Kitchens in a college. On them, notices about every conceivable thing are pinned. Glass-fronted for reasons of security.

SENT DOWN (*p.p.*): expelled, for really serious offences, or sometimes just for *folie de grandeur*.

SMALL GREEN LIGHT (*n.*) (*Oxford*): such a thing once had to be affixed to your car to prove that you were a bona fide undergraduate car driver.

SMOKER (*n.*) (*Cambridge*): bi-termly 'concert' given by the Footlights Dramatic Club.

SPORT THE OAK (*v.*): older college rooms have double doors, one outer and one inner. If you're in, you leave the outer one open; but if you're in and you don't want to be disturbed, you close it, thus giving the impression that you're out. To do this is to 'sport the oak'.

SQUARE (*n.*) (*Cambridge*): mortar board, or cap.

STAIRCASE (*n.*): the area which rooms lead off. A typical staircase will have four or five floors, with two to four sets of rooms to a floor.

STUDENT (*n.*) (*Oxford*): Fellow of Christ Church; (*anywhere else*): the person who at Oxbridge is called an undergraduate.

SUBFUSC (*n.*): academic wear for undergraduates. From the Latin *subfuscus* (*fuscus*=dark, dusky).

TOGGERS/TORPIDS (*n.*) (*Oxford*): local boat races held in February.

TOWNIE (*n.*): person of either sex who lives in Oxford or Cambridge but who has no link with the university of either town. Hence a second-class citizen.

TRINITY (*n.*): a college at both universities, and at Oxford the name of the Summer term.

TRIPOS (*n.*) (*Cambridge*): the most serious examinations (including Finals) along the way to getting your first degree.

TURL, the (*n.*) (*Oxford*): Turl Street. Former scene of battles.

UL (*n.*) (*Cambridge*): University Library. Equivalent to the Bodleian at Oxford. Both these libraries are copyright libraries, like the British Library. The UL is also remarkable for its extreme ugliness.

UNDERGRADUATE (*n.*): an Oxbrite who has not yet got even one degree.

UNION (SOCIETY) (*n.*): debating society for would-be politicos. Not to be confused with students' unions, which are usually worthy and left-wing.

UNIVERSITY (*n.*): Oxford and Cambridge are universities. The others just try to be.

VACATION (*n.*): usually abbreviated to 'vac'. Univer-

YAWNING

sity 'holidays' at Christmas, Easter and through the summer.

VICE-CHANCELLOR (*n.*): the executive boss of the university. The Chancellor is just a figurehead whom most Oxbrites never even meet.

VIVA VOCE (*n.*): usually abbreviated to 'viva', a horrific oral examination used to determine grades of degree for borderline cases. Very terrifying.

VS (*n.*) (*Oxford*): *Vix satis*. Archaic exam mark, roughly equalling a 'B'.

WC (*n.*): a form of convenience until recently unknown at Oxbridge, and still rare.

XENOPHOBIA (*n.*): not applied in its strictest sense, but a form of it is levelled at non-Oxbrites by Oxbrites.

YAWNING (*n.*): activity frequently to be observed at lectures.

ZEUGMA (*n.*): wordplay sometimes still used by would-be Oxbridge wits.

Bibliography

This is a selection only of the vast library of books on Oxbridge, and it is a selection only of those books used in the gargantuan task of assembling a true picture for this book. *All* should be studied by readers who truly wish to pass themselves off as the Genuine Article.

CAMBRIDGE

Muriel Bradbrook, *That Infidel Place*, Chatto & Windus, 1969.

Cambridge University Admissions Prospectus (for various years).

Clark, *A Concise Guide to the Town and University of Cambridge*, Bowes & Bowes, 1910

F. M. Cornford, *Microcosmographia Academica*, Bowes & Bowes, 1908.

John P. Dolan (ed.), *The Essential Erasmus*, Mentor-Omega, 1964.

Margaret Drabble, *A Summer Bird-Cage*, Penguin, 1963.

E. M. Forster, *The Longest Journey*, Penguin, 1960.

—— *Howard's End*, Penguin, 1941.

L. and H. Fowler (eds.), *Cambridge Commemorated*, CUP, 1984.

Michael Frayn, *Donkey's Years*, Methuen, 1977.

'Palinurus', *The Unquiet Grave*, Hamish Hamilton, 1945.

Gwen Raverat, *Period Piece*, Faber, 1952.

F. A. Reeve, *Cambridge*, Batsford, 1964.

S. C. Roberts, *Zuleika in Cambridge*, CUP, 1941.

Tom Sharpe, *Porterhouse Blue*, Secker & Warburg, 1974.

Andrew Sinclair, *My Friend Judas*, Penguin, 1961.

C. P. Snow, *The Masters*, Penguin, 1956.

J. V. Stevenson, *Through the Kaleidoscope*, Robin Clark, 1983.

Andrejz Zchjernowsky, *Ein Sommer in Cambridge*, Burmeister & Humperdinck, 1883.

OXFORD

Dacre Balsdon, *Oxford Life*, Eyre & Spottiswoode, 1957.

Muriel Beadle, *These Ruins are Inhabited*, Hale, 1963.

Max Beerbohm, *Zuleika Dobson*, Penguin, 1952.

John Betjeman, *An Oxford University Chest*, OUP (repr.), 1979.

Belinda Blinders, *Sandford of Merton*, ed. D. F. T. Coke, Bocardo Press, 1903.

Vera Brittain, *The Woman at Oxford*, Harrap, 1960.

J. I. Catto (ed.), *The History of Oxford*, vol. I: *The Early English Schools*, OUP, 1984.

Hal Cheetham, *Portrait of Oxford*, Hale, 1971.

The Concise Oxford Dictionary.

Michaelmas McPhee, *Un été à Oxford*, Plangent & Ivoire, 1907.

André Maurois, *Ariel*, Penguin, 1937.

Jan Morris, *Oxford*, Faber, 1965.

Jan Morris (ed.), *The Oxford Book of Oxford*, OUP, 1978.

Oxford University Admissions Prospectus (for various years).

Venables and Clifford, *Academic Dress of the University of Oxford*, OUP, 1957.

Evelyn Waugh, *Brideshead Revisited*, Chapman & Hall, 1945.

J. Wells, *The Oxford Degree Ceremony*, Clarendon Press, 1906.

A. R. Woolley, *Clarendon Guide to Oxford*, OUP, 1979.

GENERAL

Ann Barr and Peter York, *The Sloane Ranger's Handbook*, Ebury, 1982.

Oliver Lawson Dick (ed.), *Aubrey's 'Brief Lives'*, Secker & Warburg, 1949.

Mercia Mason, *Blue Guide to Oxford and Cambridge*, Benn, 1982.

James Sutherland (ed.), *The Oxford Book of Literary Anecdotes*, OUP, 1975.

Carlton Wallace (ed.), *The Schoolboy's Pocket Book*, Evans Bros, 1955.

I also owe a debt of gratitude to innumerable college and university publications across several years, notably *Varsity*, *The 1/- Paper (The 5p Paper)*, *Broadsheet*, *Stop Press*, *The Heckler*, *Granta*, *The Cambridge Review*, *Cherwell*, *Isis*, *Tributary*, the Oxford *Vade Mecum* (pub. Parchment (Oxford) Ltd), *The Oxford Handbook* (OUSU), and the *Varsity Handbook* (Varsity Publications).

Index

225

226